WISER

Books by Nicki Koziarz

5 Habits of a Woman Who Doesn't Quit

A Woman Who Doesn't Quit Bible Study

*Why Her? 6 Truths We Need to Hear When
Measuring Up Leaves Us Falling Behind*

*Rachel & Leah Bible Study: What Two Sisters
Teach Us about Combating Comparison*

Flooded: The 5 Best Decisions to Make When Life Is Hard and Doubt Is Rising

*Flooded Study Guide: The 5 Best Decisions to Make
When Life Is Hard and Doubt Is Rising*

*Your New Now: Finding Strength and Wisdom
When You Feel Stuck Where You Are*

WISER

40 Decisions to Grow
Daily in God's Wisdom

NICKI KOZIARZ

BETHANYHOUSE
a division of Baker Publishing Group
Minneapolis, Minnesota

© 2024 by Nicki Koziarz

Published by Bethany House Publishers
Minneapolis, Minnesota
BethanyHouse.com

Bethany House Publishers is a division of
Baker Publishing Group, Grand Rapids, Michigan

Printed in the United States of America

ISBN 978-0-7642-3702-7 (cloth)
ISBN 978-1-4934-4218-8 (ebook)

Library of Congress Cataloging-in-Publication Control Number: 2023037780

Devotionals 35 and 37 were previously published on Proverbs31.org.

Cover design by Alison Fargason

The author is represented by the Brock, Inc. Agency.

Baker Publishing Group publications use paper produced from sustainable forestry practices and post-consumer waste whenever possible.

24 25 26 27 28 29 30   7 6 5 4 3 2 1

To my daughters Taylor & Hope—
may God continue to make you wiser
as you lead your generation toward Truth.

CONTENTS

1

Set Yourself Apart
Each Day

Then Joshua said to the people, "Consecrate yourselves, for tomorrow the LORD will do wonders among you."

Joshua 3:5

As we made our long walk back down the gravel road that leads to our farm, I frustratedly thought, *Why are we so forgetful to close the gate to our barnyard?!*

That morning, all four of our horses had found their way out of the security of the barnyard because someone had failed to close a gate. I wish this was the first time, but it's happened multiple times.

However, this time the horses had gotten all the way to a main road. It took us over one stressful hour to catch them all.

Walking them back to a place of safety and security, all while feeling so frustrated, reminds me of what Joshua was experiencing in Joshua 3:5.

Moses died, and the leading of the Israelites had officially been passed on to him. But Joshua had been around for years, and he knew how the

Israelites could be. They were very forgetful of what God had done for them (Judges 8:34). They didn't really trust this process they were on with God, Moses, and now Joshua.

Joshua 3:5 is one of the first commands Joshua gives to the Israelites. Joshua believes in the process to protect the Israelites. But the thing I love about this command is that it reminds us:

> ## WE HAVE A PART IN GOD'S PLAN.

There are so many valuable things inside you and me that each day we let escape because of our own forgetfulness. One of the definitions of the word *consecrate* is this: to set apart.

Let's look at this from a modern lens today.

Just as God promised Israel He would do wonders through them, God has promised the same for us today. God has good things planned. And even if God never did another thing for us, there are things you and I could recount today as a testimony of His faithfulness.

But for us to stay expectant for all the things to come, there is a daily need to set ourselves apart. But—like how remembering to close the gate is such a struggle for my family—we often forget how important time with God is.

Carpool must get rolling, your boss emailed you an urgent request, the house is a mess, and a dozen other things fight for us to forget our most valuable asset: time with God.

But today, as you are investing in your day by reading this devotion, you are making the decision to set yourself apart for God's glory.

We have a part in God's plan. Let's take this seriously and do the work our souls need to be set apart.

TAKE THIS DEVOTION DEEPER

What are the things fighting for your attention right now?

What does it look like for you to say no to those things and yes to spending time with God?

Read Psalm 86:11 and write out what you think having an undivided heart means.

2

Stand Firm So That "None of These Things" Will Move You Today

But none of these things move me, neither count I my life dear unto myself, so that I might finish my course with joy, and the ministry, which I have received of the Lord Jesus, to testify the gospel of the grace of God.

Acts 20:24 KJV

I want you to think of the last really bad day you had. I know, not super encouraging. But seriously, take a minute and think about it.

What were the events that happened?

How did you react to each of those situations?

And what were the words you spoke on that day?

The last really bad day I had was just a few months ago.

A teacher called me about something one of my kids had done in her class, and it was the kind of situation that makes you want to resign from motherhood. A few minutes later, a friend texted me a picture she thought was hysterical that she had taken of me. It wasn't funny to me, and seeing myself like that made me irritated with her.

Then my husband came home and threw the mail on the counter—a big, unexpected bill. And to end the day, I lost an opportunity for work, which made the unexpected bill feel even more stressful.

The truth was that my circumstances were moving my faith to a place I didn't want to be.

Paul, the speaker in Acts 20:24, knew something about bad days. His days, though, were harder than what most of us would consider a bad day.

But one of the reasons Paul was able to declare "But none of these things move me" was because Paul had been given the opportunity to see heaven. He understood that anything that would happen here on this earth didn't really matter because, in what would feel like just a minute, we would be in heaven.

> **WE WILL HAVE HARD, BAD DAYS.**
> **BUT IT'S JUST A BAD DAY, NOT A BAD LIFE.**

Like Paul, we can make the decision to believe that although these things here on earth are hard, irritating, or just inconvenient, that doesn't mean we have to be shaken by them.

Make the decision today that no matter what comes your way, your faith and hope in Jesus will not be moved. It's setting the enemy on notice. He can try to defeat and discourage you, but he will not win.

TAKE THIS DEVOTION DEEPER

Paul frequently used the metaphor of running a race to describe his faith.

Look up these other references to this concept:
1 Corinthians 9:24
Galatians 5:7
Philippians 3:13–14
2 Timothy 4:7

What does it look like for you today to run your race well?

Why do you think that sometimes a bad day can send us on a downward emotional and mental spiral?

3

MAKE THE DECISION TO

Keep Your Words in Line with Your Heart

May these words of my mouth and this meditation of my heart be pleasing in your sight, LORD, my Rock and my Redeemer.

Psalm 19:14 NIV

My friend and I hadn't seen each other in a few weeks, so I was excited to catch up on her life. After arriving at the restaurant, we hugged, took our seats, and ordered some chips and salsa. Immediately we started talking about what had been going on in our lives and dug into a discussion about the previous month's events.

A person's name (who I didn't care for) came up a few minutes into our catch-up session. My friend told me a story that made me dislike this person even more. I then told my friend a story about this person that made her dislike them more.

And so our conversation went.

When I left the restaurant, there was a convicting feeling inside me. My thoughts wandered through our conversation, and I felt deeply bothered that it'd been nothing but idle talk.

The interesting thing was, during the conversation, I didn't even realize what was happening. I thought I was just catching up with an old friend. But the reality was, my heart and my words were not in line.

I had just recently read Psalm 19:14, which I believe is one of the greatest verses of inspiration when it comes to this daily decision we can make. During biblical times, when someone was going to bring an animal sacrifice to the temple, the priest would inspect it to see if it was blemish-free (see Leviticus 1:1–17). If it was not blemish-free, the animal and the person were both rejected by the priest.

So as David penned these words in Psalm 19, he most likely had this image in his mind.

There are so many things that make our hearts messy before God. But as followers of Jesus, once we receive the gift of salvation, we are clean before God.

> **GOD ALWAYS WELCOMES US, NOT BECAUSE OF ANYTHING WE HAVE DONE BUT SOLELY BASED ON HIS SACRIFICE ON THE CROSS.**

But the reality is, most of us struggle daily to have our hearts—made clean because of Jesus—reflected in our words. Because it's so easy to slip into gossip and negative talk or to speak things of others that reflect the opposite of this grace in our lives.

I wish I could tell you this eye-opening moment changed me, and I never spoke badly of someone again. But I am a woman who consistently finds herself in need of God's grace, mercy, and forgiveness. I'm sure you understand what this is like.

The truth is, I'm grateful I left that conversation with a conviction to make a confession that the words of my mouth were not in line with the salvation of my heart. It is a daily decision to make sure my heart is aligned with God, so my words follow suit.

It's a daily step toward us becoming wiser.

God doesn't require perfection from any of us. But He does remind us throughout Scripture that this is a decision we need to intentionally make.

TAKE THIS DEVOTION DEEPER

Write out Psalm 19:14 three times below and make a commitment to memorize this verse. Circle the words that stand out the most to you and pray this verse over your life.

1.

2.

3.

4

Want to Understand the Bible More

All Scripture is breathed out by God and profitable for teaching, for reproof, for correction, and for training in righteousness.

2 Timothy 3:16

For the past few months, I've been trying to learn something new. My husband and I own a small farm just outside of Charlotte, North Carolina. Not long ago, a rescued horse found his forever home with us.

I knew a little about horses but not enough to train and work with him. I asked around and came across a woman who has spent her entire life with horses. She's essentially the horse whisperer, and everyone around our little area knows her, even the horses.

The first time she pulled up to our white barn to meet me and my horse, Tennessee, I asked her how many lessons it would take for me to really get a grasp on working with him. I thought maybe three or four.

She laughed—not to mock me but to dispel my overachiever, naïve sense of this learning process.

That was about twenty lessons ago, and I still have a long way to go to learn what I need to learn.

I think you'd agree that learning to do new things is challenging. As children, we enter into new things with that unstoppable sense of belief that we can do anything! But then, after some years of failure and frustration in our lives, taking the chance on learning something new is hard.

And so, we think, *Why bother?*

Sometimes studying the Bible feels this way. There is so much to learn and understand, and often we just don't think we're smart enough to study the Bible on our own.

We can lose our motivation to study because things get complicated in our minds.

Second Timothy 3:16 gives us a good dose of motivation to stay in a posture of wanting to learn new things about the Bible: "All Scripture is breathed out by God and profitable for teaching, for reproof, for correction, and for training in righteousness."

When Paul wrote this letter to Timothy, his mentee, Paul was explaining that it is a blessing to understand the Word of God. In fact, the things he mentions in this one verse are all powerful reminders to stay motivated to keep learning.

Making a decision to learn more about Scripture helps us learn more about God because, as Paul reminds us, these are God's breath-inspired words. Learning more about Scripture teaches us how to persevere in life. For every hard and trying situation we will face, there's someone in the Bible we can learn from through their process with God.

Making a decision to learn to ride a horse and learning to study the Bible aren't exactly the same. But both require a commitment to the process and a plan to press on, even when we feel frustrated or don't understand everything.

I had to find someone to teach me to work with Tennessee. And guess what?

> WE HAVE A TEACHER, THE HOLY SPIRIT, READY
> TO HELP US UNDERSTAND GOD'S WORD.
> INVITING HIM INTO OUR STUDY AND LEARNING
> PROCESS IS PURPOSEFUL AND POWERFUL.

Today, we can start with this posture in our hearts and simply ask the Holy Spirit to show us something new about the Bible.

But the decision is ours to make. May we decide today to take the time to understand the Bible more.

TAKE THIS DEVOTION DEEPER

What are some questions you have about studying the Bible? Write them in the space below:

Pray and ask the Holy Spirit to guide you to a person, a book, or a resource to help you find the answers to those questions.

5

Stop Replaying the Negative

Finally, brothers, whatever is true, whatever is honorable, whatever is just, whatever is pure, whatever is lovely, whatever is commendable, if there is any excellence, if there is anything worthy of praise, think about these things.

Philippians 4:8

Recently, I was watching a streaming show that was doing some social experiments. One of the experiments fascinated me. Participants were told they were going to perform spinning a plate on a stick and that there would be someone in the room giving them feedback.

But they didn't know that the feedback was random; some would be positive (even if they were bad at it), and some would be negative (even if they were good at it). After they received their feedback, they would have a few more hours to practice and come back and perform again.

I really thought the participants with the *negative feedback* would go out, practice even harder, and come back and do amazing. Because that's what I would do.

But I was so wrong.

Those with *positive feedback*, even if they weren't super talented at the plate spinning, came back and did amazing. Those with *negative feedback*, even if they were talented at spinning the plate, came back and did horribly.

I started to think about an area in my life that I had lost my passion and drive to be better in. And I very quickly realized I was replaying so much negative feedback over that area of my life, and I was getting worse at it.

But God challenged me with Philippians 4:8.

> **THIS VERSE ISN'T ABOUT WISHFUL THINKING. IT'S ABOUT LEARNING TO TRAIN OUR BRAINS TO THINK LIKE GOD WANTS US TO THINK.**

He doesn't want us to dwell on things we can't change or unhealthy patterns that only see the negative.

With the Holy Spirit's prompting, I sat down and wrote ten things people had said positive things about in an area of my life where I was looking for negative feedback. I asked God to help me rewrite a new narrative that would help make me better at this thing I was struggling with.

And after just a few times of doing this with God, my passion came back, my hopes were high again, and slowly but surely, I got better at what I was doing.

Today's decision is to think about positive feedback over negative. It's one of the wisest decisions you can make for your life, because negative replays and negative thinking only waste your brain space and energy.

I want you to think about something you may have lost your passion for or something that looks hopeless in your life. Are there negative words and stories attached to that thing? If so, you and God may have some work to do together to get to a better space in your life.

You'll see space for you to write out ten positive things people have said about something you may be losing your passion for. You may not be able to write all ten, but try to at least get to five today. Anytime you feel yourself slipping into that negative space in your mind, go back to that list and pray this:

God, lead my thoughts right now to a place that is true, honorable, just, pure, lovely, commendable, excellent, and worthy of praise. Help me remember today that I decided to stop replaying the negative. Amen.

TAKE THIS DEVOTION DEEPER

Read all of Philippians 4.

Write out ten positive things someone has said about you.

10 Positive Things Someone Has Said about Me

1.

2.

3.

4.

5.

6.

7.

8.

9.

10.

6

See Yourself and Others As Valuable

Do nothing out of selfish ambition or vain conceit. Rather, in humility value others above yourselves.

Philippians 2:3 NIV

A few months ago, I had to have a semihard conversation with a friend. I say semihard because this friend and I have the kind of relationship where we can say what we need to say and move on. But still, it wasn't fun.

She was struggling because someone had started a business similar to hers. And this other person had a good following, a respectable reputation, and decent potential to have a thriving business.

And my friend admittedly felt threatened.

But she didn't just feel threatened, she started *acting* threatened.

A sense of panic rushed over her as she verbally weighed all the possibilities of what could happen with this new business scenario. For several days, I watched her wrestle through a roller coaster of jealous emotions.

Each time she would say something about this new business owner, I would take a deep breath as my stomach twisted and turned. I knew

I needed to say something, but I didn't want to hurt her already fragile spirit.

So one afternoon, while we were on the phone discussing this other business, I gently walked her through all the reasons her business was awesome. I reassured her I was with her, but then I said something really hard: "You gotta let her be her and you be you. You are both called and chosen to do this assignment. Not either-or. But this anxiety you feel . . . it has the potential to ruin you."

I don't think it's what she wanted me to say in that moment, but it's what she needed me to say.

I know, because I needed someone to say it to me years ago when I walked through a similar situation. I let being threatened by someone else's success ruin days and weeks of my life. And it took what seemed like forever to get over it.

I had to decide to see myself as valuable but also to see her the same way.

Here's the thing: I know what she's doing looks awesome. And she makes it look effortless. And maybe she can do it better. But she is also called, chosen, and set apart by God for a purpose.

And so are you.

One thing I've come to understand about God is He's got enough purpose and potential to go around.

> ## GOD'S PURPOSE ISN'T A BATTLEFIELD FOR COMPETITION; IT'S A SAFE HAVEN OF CALLING.

The secret to doing something confidently (yet humbly) for God?
Be with Jesus.
Humility is the by-product of His presence flowing in our lives.

When we are in His presence, He gives us the confidence to believe we are created to do something great with our lives. His presence whispers assurance over our souls when we feel vulnerable.

And His presence gives us the ability to cheer on that girl next to us, no matter how threatened we feel.

I need Philippians 2:3 to help me make the decision to recognize that God values humility with the gifts and talents He's given me. My gifts are not to make myself better than the girl next to me. And because of this verse, I'm reminded to value what she's doing even more than what I'm doing.

My friend and I are both still working through this struggle each day. Neither one of us has perfected humble confidence. But we are both trying our best to put our insecurities to the side each day and run fiercely toward the process of godly success.

TAKE THIS DEVOTION DEEPER

Who is an example of someone in your life who feels like a threat?

Let's go ahead and make today's decision now.

- Write out the ways you see yourself as valuable as it pertains to this situation.

- Then, write out the ways the other person is valuable, too.

7

MAKE THE DECISION TO
Ask the Right Questions
for Direction

Get all the advice and instruction you can, so you will be wise the rest of your life.

Proverbs 19:20 NLT

Sometimes we find ourselves in situations where it feels impossible to have wisdom, direction, and discernment about what to do next. Which is exactly how I felt that morning.

There wasn't anything tragically wrong. I hadn't gone through a major life change, but I just didn't know what step to take next as I looked at my to-do list of prayed-through possibilities.

I sat at my simple white desk in my office with bright white walls and big windows. The simplicity and light of this room normally fill me with peace as I work. But sudden anxiety made this bright space seem as if a dark cloud quickly moved to cover the brightness.

It brought to mind all the questions:

What if I get the next step wrong?
What if I miss what God has for me?
What if I am not brave enough to do what I need to do next?

It's often these questions we ask ourselves that lead to the greatest thoughts of doubt, discouragement, and defeat.

> ## BUT THERE'S A SAYING:
> ## "SHOW ME YOUR FRIENDS,
> ## AND I'LL SHOW YOU YOUR FUTURE."

It reminds me of this verse: "Get all the advice and instruction you can, so you will be wise the rest of your life" (Proverbs 19:20 NLT). As we surround ourselves with people who reflect God, their wisdom can help guide us toward our next step.

So, I texted the wisest friend I know and asked if I could get her perspective about the things on my list. Instead of texting back what she thought I should do, she asked me three important questions.

Questions that helped me change the way I was looking at the list.

Questions I want to share with you if you're also in a season of seeking.

Questions that offer the chance to reflect godly wisdom and I hope encourage you, too.

Question One: Who are the people you are here for?

This is important because we can start to think we're here for everyone, all the time. But the reality is, there's a burden God has placed inside you for a specific set of people here on this earth. Figure out who they are, and then . . .

Question Two: What are you supposed to give them?

Each of us has a unique gift to bring to this world. The people you're here for need what you have to give them. Whether it be time, encouragement, prayer, teaching, or a dozen other possibilities, never think this world has everything it needs. It needs what you have to give.

Question Three: What gives you the most energy when you put energy into it?

There are certain things we have to do in life that don't necessarily feel life-giving, and yet we have to do them anyway. But your God assignments should make you feel like you're alive and ready to do them again and again and again.

I let these three questions turn into prayers. And slowly, God started to reveal where to direct my focus on that list of possibilities.

He is ready to do the same for you. You can have clarity. You can have a sense of direction. And you can trust the process of finding wisdom in your life by making the decision to ask yourself the right questions rather than circling in endless questioning thoughts.

And if you don't believe that just yet, I believe it for you.

TAKE THIS DEVOTION DEEPER

In the space below, answer those three questions the best you can:

1. Who are the people you are here for?

2. What are you supposed to give them?

3. What gives you the most energy when you put energy into it?

8

MAKE THE DECISION TO

Look for Evidence of God's Faithfulness

Let us hold fast the confession of our hope without wavering, for he who promised is faithful.

Hebrews 10:23

If you've felt like this season of life has been uncomfortable and unfamiliar, you are not alone.

If you've wondered what God is doing in this season, you are not alone. And if you've struggled to find anything that feels normal, you are not alone.

Lately, life has felt hard and ever-changing. There is a fear inside many of us as we wonder if life will ever feel normal again and crave that which feels familiar.

I'll be honest. The circumstances, pain, loss, and disorder our world has experienced in recent months have left me feeling like it's all exceeding the plan of God's goodness.

But I know this isn't true. And I'm sure you do, too. We often find ourselves (falsely) believing that what we see is what we should feel. So when we see darkness, we feel darkness. We see gloom, and we feel gloom. When we see hopelessness, we feel hopeless.

The book of Hebrews was written to be a source of encouragement for the Jews in Jerusalem who experienced persecution for their belief in God. Their faith had been flipped upside down, and nothing felt normal to them either.

They were craving God's familiar faithfulness, and the writer of this verse was trying to remind them of this sacred One who never leaves us.

This is one of the many reasons I love the Word of God, because for every hard thing we will walk through on this earth, there's someone who walked through it before us. As we study the Bible, we see the wisdom, encouragement, and truth that apply to us today.

And this is why we can declare Hebrews 10:23 for our lives right now: "Let us hold fast the confession of our hope without wavering, for he who promised is faithful." Tucked in this verse is the promise of God's familiar faithfulness—both then and today.

Seasons may come and go, but His familiar faithfulness remains.

> **LIFE WILL TWIST AND TURN, BUT WE CAN ALWAYS SEE GOD'S FAMILIAR FAITHFULNESS IF WE DECIDE TO LOOK FOR IT.**

God cannot lie, He never changes His mind, He never forgets His Word, and He has never failed anyone with the fulfillment of His promises. Jesus's death and resurrection never stop existing. It's up to us to look for the familiar faithfulness of God in seasons that feel uncomfortable, unfamiliar, and ever-changing.

Our news feeds will always be filled with heartache, hard situations, and heavy struggles in our world. It might make us question His faithfulness, but we can still find it through the pages of our Bible.

There is a fresh wind of grace flowing into our lives today through the Holy Spirit. It's not stale, old, or even normal. But it is familiar. And as we worship, praise, and declare His faithfulness over our lives, that wind will feel stronger and stronger.

Today's decision is to look for evidence of God's faithfulness. How will we do this?

First, we must be willing to admit our own shortcomings in these faith struggles. Repent, and ask God to forgive you. Do this in the space below:

Next, it's time for us to look back and remember the times we've seen God show us His faithfulness in the past. Use the spaces below and write out five times in your life you've seen God come through for you.

1.

2.

3.

4.

5.

Now, we bring our worries, concerns, and fears about whether or not we believe God is going to come through for us. Use this next section to write out anything you are worried about experiencing God's faithfulness in:

And last, before you fall asleep tonight, write down one way you saw God's faithfulness, and declare this as your decision to find God's faithfulness today:

TAKE THIS DEVOTION DEEPER

Look up the following verses about the evidence of God's faithfulness and write each of them out.

1. Lamentations 3:22–23

2. 1 Corinthians 1:9

3. Psalm 26:3

9

MAKE THE DECISION TO
Remember Who Your Battle Is Against

The Lord says to my Lord: "Sit at my right hand, until I make your enemies your footstool."

Psalm 110:1

One of my favorite things about social media is how quickly something can be shared, again and again. It makes me smile when I see people sharing each other's posts because they believe someone else needs to see it. We often see the hashtag #repost when things are shared this way.

But sometimes social media can feel like the enemy, digging up things from the past to turn us against each other.

I had this happen not long ago.

Years before a certain political leader was elected to their position, I had attended a nonpolitical event where a friend of mine was being nominated for special recognition. We had taken a picture with this person who was there presenting the awards, long before they were in any type of political role. I posted it because I was proud of my friend.

But after a few years passed, the award presenter was now in a highly controversial political role, and I completely forgot about the post. During this time, people were looking for anything to turn someone against them, and someone found my post and reposted it as an attempt to slam my character.

Sometimes social media is a great way to spread something, and other times it feels like a weapon we use to make enemies.

If social media had been around when the Bible was being written, the hashtag #repost could have easily been used along with the verse Psalm 110:1 in a good way. This verse was used repeatedly throughout Scripture, and biblical heroes loved to share it.

Here are a few examples:

- Jesus quoted Psalm 110:1 in Matthew 22:43–45 and Mark 12:36–37.
- Peter quoted Psalm 110:1 in Acts 2:34–35.
- Paul referenced Psalm 110:1 in 1 Corinthians 15:25.

Why was it quoted so much?

Because this is a Messianic psalm, meaning it points to the prophecy and fulfillment of Jesus Christ. One of the things I think we often forget when studying Scripture is that we're not through the entire story of God—*yet.*

There are still prophecies in Scripture that will be fulfilled. The enemies of God being put in their place forever is a prime example.

We're still awaiting the redemptive day evil has no influence. Even though that day is yet to come, and we can see so much evidence of that on social media, there is so much to hold on to through this verse.

The right hand of God is the place of honor and authority. When Jesus died on the cross, Scripture tells us He was taken up to heaven and seated at the right hand of God (Mark 16:19).

So the first part of Psalm 110:1 has been fulfilled. Jesus is seated at the right hand of God. This also means that through salvation in Christ we have full access to the Father. We can trust we are safe and secure despite the evil that seems to prevail.

But what about the second part of Psalm 110:1?

It's coming. We're still awaiting the day when the enemies of God become a footstool at the feet of Jesus. But that doesn't mean redemption hasn't already begun (Ephesians 1:7).

> ## THE ENEMIES OF GOD ARE TEMPORARY BECAUSE JESUS IS IN HIS PERMANENT PLACE.

As humans, it's so easy for us to want to do something in the midst of a battle. I wanted to fire back a post at that person who was trying to slam me online. But I've come to understand our battles are not against each other: there is a dark force of the enemies of God trying to divide us, God's people.

What if the decision we made today was to come back to this verse, this promise, this prophecy? We can decide to understand that our enemies are not each other. God is our defender. And He is not finished.

Billy Graham said at one of his 1975 revivals in New Mexico, "I've read the last page of the Bible; I know it's going to come out all right."[1]

Sometimes just believing that is enough to remind us what this is all about.

TAKE THIS DEVOTION DEEPER

Read all of Psalm 110. Then, do a short study on the other places we mentioned this verse is found:

Matthew 22:43–45

Mark 12:36–37

Acts 2:34–35

1 Corinthians 15:25

10

MAKE THE DECISION TO

Look for the Goodness of God

We destroy arguments and every lofty opinion raised against the knowledge of God, and take every thought captive to obey Christ.

2 Corinthians 10:5

I'm not a psychologist or licensed counselor. But I knew something was spiritually and emotionally unhealthy in me a few months ago. Day after day, I began to wake up with this same gloomy feeling over me.

When I would open up my emails, news apps, and social media accounts, there I would see it: gloom.

It felt unavoidable, and it was all I could see everywhere I turned. At the same time, in doing research for a project I was working on, I came across a term called *confirmation bias*.

According to the *Oxford English Dictionary*, the definition of confirmation bias is "the tendency to seek or favour new information which supports one's existing theories or beliefs."[1]

Plainly put, this means what we believe inside us becomes what we look for around us. Evidence. Proof. Justification for our feelings.

I realized very quickly that I had written a story for the current state of my life. One that was filled with sad days, hard situations, and . . . gloom. I was experiencing confirmation bias because I would wake up each day and subconsciously look for gloom.

And I found it.

But once I understood what confirmation bias was, I became challenged to change.

Even if life is trying to write a story of gloom, we are followers of Jesus. And the story Jesus left for us is one of hope, power, and might. Yet, Jesus never said this would be easy. And I think we can all agree, it's not.

Second Corinthians 10:5 is one of my favorite verses because it's practical wisdom for our lives.

Even though this was written so long ago, Paul is normalizing our daily battle of the mind. He tells us we should take every thought captive and make it obedient to Christ.

Thoughts that are obedient to Christ are always based on the hope He gives us. But this can be a hard process because, honestly, I feel like the way our lives have been challenged lately has rewired us to expect gloom.

> **BUT WHAT WE BELIEVE**
> **IS OFTEN WHAT WE BECOME.**

Today, I want to challenge you the same way I've challenged myself these last few months. Make a decision to read 2 Corinthians 10:5 a few times and let Paul's God-breathed wisdom shift something in you.

After you read it, pray and ask the Lord to show you how you can replace the gloom of life with the perspective of the goodness of God.

Then, look for evidence all day of things that are lovely, commendable, excellent, and worthy of praise. If you're struggling to see them, ask the Holy Spirit to help you.

By doing this, we will start to see evidence of opportunities in the midst of opposition. Faithfulness that is not covered up by frustrations. Beauty from brokenness. Gratitude instead of grief. And the power of God despite the problems of man.

What you see is what you'll get.

TAKE THIS DEVOTION DEEPER

Using the space below, write out at least five ways you've seen the goodness of God in your life or the lives of others recently:

1.

2.

3.

4.

5.

11

Believe That God Can and Will Use You Just As You Are

Jesus replied, "What is impossible with man is possible with God."

Luke 18:27 NIV

I t was my senior year of high school. The grass was turning greener, birds chirping louder, and department stores were lining their racks with beautiful formal gowns.

Spring had sprung, and that meant just one thing to a senior girl: prom.

I took my seat in my homeroom class and began working on the previous night's history assignment. The bell dinged, and the redundant morning announcements blasted over the loudspeaker. I didn't pay much attention until I heard, "Today in every homeroom class you will need to nominate this year's prom king and queen."

Suddenly my stomach was tangled in knots. I knew never to get my hopes up. After all, I was the athletic girl who was at church every time the doors opened, not the socialite this honor required. While I knew not to expect it, inside I still wanted to be worthy of being prom queen.

I couldn't shake the dreadful feeling as sheets of paper were passed around the room for us to write down our nominations. *Would my name be on any of them?*

It wouldn't take long to find out. Our teacher took his place front and center in the classroom. As he collected the papers, he called out the names written down. I waited on pins and needles. Thirty seconds before the bell rang, we nominated that year's prom king and queen.

Quickly I made my way to the only place a girl can get an ounce of privacy in a large high school: the bathroom. I shut the rusted stall door and wept.

It wasn't me . . . again. No one picked me. I was forever an unlikely prom queen candidate.

That moment was defining. Looking back, I can see that I started to become unlikely in a different way.

It could have ruined me—and in a way it did. For good. You see, I discovered in Scripture there are many who didn't meet the qualifications of society: great heroes of faith who were improbable candidates. Men and women who faced impossible odds with the God of all possibilities.

Moses was not an eloquent speaker, but he met with God and delivered the Ten Commandments to a generation of people (Exodus 19–20). David was an adulterer but is described as a man after God's heart (1 Kings 14:8, Acts 13:22). The Samaritan woman was a repeat sinner, but her testimony led her entire community to see Jesus (John 4). Jesus's very own disciple Peter denied Him three times, but he went on to be the rock of the Church (Matthew 16:18).

God seemed to have handpicked and set apart these unlikely people. He used each of them for a redemptive purpose, despite their inadequacies. And turned their impossible into possible.

I'm finding this is exactly what God wants to do through my own flawed life. He wants me to make the decision to believe He can and will use me just as I am.

Is there something in your past that you feel is too far a stretch for God to use? Do you possess a quality that the world would look at and say, "Nope, not you"? Have you ever felt completely unqualified but still dream of doing impossible things?

If so, you should get ready.

> ## GOD QUALIFIES THE UNQUALIFIED, AND HE DEEMS THE UNLIKELY LIKELY.

Never think your inadequacies are too much for Him.

He's called you. He's chosen you. Make the decision to believe, "What is impossible with man is possible with God" (Luke 18:27 NIV). God can and will use you just as you are.

TAKE THIS DEVOTION DEEPER

What are a few inadequacies you see in yourself that you struggle to believe God could use?

Look up these confidence-building verses and read them aloud:

John 10:10
1 Corinthians 1:25
2 Corinthians 12:9

12

MAKE THE DECISION TO
Stay with God

But Ruth replied, "Don't urge me to leave you or to turn back from you.
Where you go I will go, and where you stay I will stay. Your people will
be my people and your God my God."

Ruth 1:16 NIV

Have you ever gone through a shattered season of life?

I found myself there in the early years of my marriage. My husband was hospitalized for two weeks and lost his job. Our oldest daughter had a very expensive surgery, a new baby was on the way, and we lost our home due to medical expenses. Each way I turned it seemed life was falling apart.

I felt hopeless and broken for a long time.

But what is so powerful about God's Word is it teaches us that even in the midst of tragedy, God is faithful. The book of Ruth is a powerful example of this.

The first few verses of the book of Ruth introduce us to an Israelite family: Elimelek, Naomi, and their two sons, Mahlon and Kilion. They were living in Bethlehem, the same place where Jesus would be born about one thousand years later.

Because of a famine, Elimelek made the decision to move his family to a place called Moab, where there was food and work. However, Moab was a dangerous place for an Israelite family because of the Moabites.

The Israelites worshiped God—Jehovah. But the Moabites worshiped a god named Chemosh. This false god represented some horrific things. These two religions were like oil and water, not very mixable.

In Ruth 1:1 it says Elimelek went to live in the country of Moab. In Hebrew, the word *live* means a sojourn or temporary stay. You see, Elimelek had no intentions of Moab becoming a permanent home.

But what he didn't know was that this temporary stay would soon become a place of permanent pain.

In the course of time, the two sons married Moabite women named Orpah and Ruth, and not long after, tragedy unfolds. First Elimelek died, then Mahlon and Killion died, leaving three widows and no children (Ruth 1:3, 5). This widowed and childless scenario left these three women, Naomi, Orpah, and Ruth, in a place of near hopelessness.

A shattered season? Definitely.

But tragedy doesn't exempt us from the need to make decisions. And so, three decisions were made.

The first decision: Naomi

She made a decision to go back to the one place she had any ounce of hope left: Bethlehem (Ruth 1:6). Naomi begged the girls not to go with her. In fact, she practically demanded they return to their families and their god.

The second decision: Orpah

She made a decision to obey Naomi's request and flee to what was familiar, her family and her god (Ruth 1:14).

The third decision: Ruth

She made the decision to stay with Naomi (Ruth 1:16–18).

I wondered what would cause Ruth to do the opposite of Orpah and decide to stay with Naomi. But in Ruth 1:16, when Ruth says, "Your God will be my God . . ." we see a little insight behind Ruth's decision to stay.

When Ruth committed to returning to Bethlehem with Naomi, there was no promise of stability or a good future. Ruth had no idea what was ahead; she just made the decision to stay—stay with Naomi and stay with God, no matter what.

> WHAT IF WE OFFERED GOD
> THIS SAME TYPE OF COMMITMENT?
> THAT WE'LL STAY WITH HIM WHEN IT'S GOOD.
> WE'LL STAY WITH HIM WHEN IT'S HARD.
> WE'LL STAY WITH HIM WHEN IT'S EASY,
> AND WE'LL STAY WITH HIM
> WHEN IT'S COMPLICATED.

That shattered season I walked through was painful. Like Ruth, I never knew what was ahead. But I knew I needed God. Staying with God showed me a dozen examples of His faithfulness. Like the time the pantry was getting bare and a food basket was anonymously set on our front doorstep that same night. It was a small sign of hope that God would see us through.

And as we make this decision to stay with God, no matter what, we'll see His faithfulness, too. May we not give in to the temptation to give up on God.

Stay with God.

Pray this with me today as we make this decision:

God, thank You for the reminder that You see us through shattered seasons. I want to be someone who stays with You. Even when it's hard, messy, or complicated, help me to lean into You. Today, I commit to stay. In Jesus's name, amen.

TAKE THIS DEVOTION DEEPER

Read the entire book of Ruth; it's only four chapters, you can do it! Something I really like to do when getting an overview of a text in the Bible is to listen to it being read to me. You can use an app like YouVersion to do this.

As you listen to or read the book of Ruth, write down the ways you see Ruth follow through with this decision to stay with God:

13

MAKE THE DECISION TO
Put Your Feet with Your Faith

He will cover you with his feathers, and under his wings you will find refuge; his faithfulness will be your shield and rampart.

Psalm 91:4 NIV

I wasn't familiar with prayer walks, but somehow, I knew they were something I needed to do.

My daughter attended a school where a horrible event took place at the end of the school year. Thousands of people were impacted by this incredibly tragic situation.

Sadly, we see these tragic stories played out regularly. Every day we leave our homes and enter places and spaces where we know we could encounter such unthinkable acts of evil.

Concern, worry, and fear filled me as the calendar flipped the page to the week before school started again.

So, I had a decision to make: sit with fear or put my feet to my faith, literally.

I chose the second option.

Texting my friend, who is a faithful prayer warrior and the mom of a student at the same school, I asked if she was up for a prayer walk across the school campus.

She was in and texted a few others to join us.

Scripture doesn't specifically reference prayer walking, but 1 Thessalonians 5:17 instructs us to "pray without ceasing." And in Joshua 6, we read about the Israelites walking around the city of Jericho to see the city walls fall down so they could enter the promised land God had given them.

Based on that passage in Joshua and 1 Thessalonians 5:17, I can't help but think there's a connection between our feet and our faith.

In our easily distracted culture, prayer walks can become a tool to help us fix our faith on one place. Whether at a school, neighborhood, or community area, prayer walking can be a focused way to help us pray.

So, on the Sunday night before school resumed after the horrible event, we made our way to the campus with our battle plan:

Prayer.

Prayer.

And . . . prayer.

We printed off Psalm 91 to use as our guide:

We prayed for God's place of refuge to feel real on that campus (Psalm 91:2).

We prayed for discernment, for eyes to see things that need to be seen (Psalm 91:3).

We prayed for God's shield to be known (Psalm 91:4).

We prayed for peace over the anxiety the students and staff would feel as they returned to the campus (Psalm 91:5–6).

We prayed that those who would call upon the name of the Lord for protection would experience it (Psalm 91:14–16).

After our feet had faithfully stepped across most of the campus, our group stood in one final prayer circle. We held hands and declared one more time the protection of God over the vicinity.

Then the neatest thing happened.

As we said *Amen*, one tiny white feather floated into the center of our circle. It reminded me of our verse today, Psalm 91:4 (NIV), and an overwhelming sense of peace stirred inside me: "He will cover you with his feathers, and under his wings you will find refuge; his faithfulness will be your shield and rampart." No matter what would come, we knew God was with us.

What if today—during a lunch break, when walking the kids to the park, or while out running errands—we used that time to make a decision to put our feet with our faith? What if we all did prayer walks?

It's free and quick and you don't even need anyone with you. Just pick an area you feel led to pray over and head that way. You can find a few verses to pray or use Psalm 91 as your guide.

As your feet press the ground and your prayers go up, declare God's promises will come down on this very broken world. Speak the name of Jesus again and again. Read Scripture. And believe there is security and hope in seeking His presence where evil has tried to prevail.

> **PRAYING BOLDLY OVER AN AREA OF OUR LIFE ISN'T A GUARANTEE NOTHING BAD WILL EVER HAPPEN THERE AGAIN, BUT IT'S A CONFIDENCE IN KNOWING OUR GOD IS WATCHING OVER THAT AREA, AND HE HEARS OUR PRAYERS.**

We might never see on this side of eternity what our prayers do, but they are doing something. And that is something every wise woman believes.

TAKE THIS DEVOTION DEEPER

Read 1 Thessalonians 5:17.

Decide to do a prayer walk using the guided prompts below:

1. Pray and ask the Holy Spirit to show you where to do a prayer walk.
2. Go to NickiKoziarz.com/Freebies and print the resource "See-over prayers." This is based on Psalm 91.
3. Make a decision about when you will do your prayer walk and who you want to invite.

I'm doing my prayer walk on . . .

with . . .

at this place . . .

14

Listen to Trusted Wisdom and Guidance from Others

> Elisha sent a messenger to say to him, "Go, wash yourself seven times in the Jordan, and your flesh will be restored and you will be cleansed."
>
> 2 Kings 5:10 NIV

Have you ever heard someone say, "God told me to do this," and thought it sounded strange?

We live in a need-to-make-sense-of-things world. We want explanations, almost instantly, for everything. So, it can feel like a stretch to try to make sense of the ways God often leads us to obey. Especially when those instructions come from someone else.

In the first verse of 2 Kings 5, we see quite the description of a man named Naaman. He was a commander, a great man, highly regarded, and a valiant soldier. And then, there's this *but*: ". . . but he had leprosy" (2 Kings 5:1 NIV).

What started in private, a little spot showing up on his body, a secret, turned his life into a public undeserved shame. Not only was leprosy a very painful disease, but society treated you horribly. No one spoke to you. You lived alone. And without a miracle, you would die a slow, painful death.

Naaman had some skepticism about Elisha's instructions. But he was desperate. And when our most significant moments of desperation lead us into the presence of the Deliverer, it is the best place to go.

So Naaman went to see Elisha, this amazing prophet he had heard had done some incredible miracles. The same kind of miracles we would later see Jesus do.

Including healing people from leprosy (Luke 17:11–19).

Elisha, through a messenger, gives Naaman some specific instructions in order to be healed (2 Kings 5:10). These instructions seem too strange and humbling for a man like Naaman to do.

Naaman had his own vision of what this miracle should look like—a simple waving of the hand over his body would do just fine for his miracle (2 Kings 5:11).

Don't we do this, too? We know God can do something, but we want it done the way that makes sense to us. And when it doesn't make sense—when it feels strange—obedience is tough.

Thankfully, God will often place people around us who can speak the truth to us in our desperate moments. But it will become a decision for us to make as to whether or not we welcome wisdom from others.

For Naaman, this came from an unlikely source—his servants. This is a reminder to us to never discount someone because of their status.

> ## IN GOD'S EYES,
> ## WE'RE ALL ABLE TO BE TRUTH GIVERS.

Finally, Naaman takes the advice of his servants and does what Elisha instructed. And he is healed and overwhelmed with gratitude (2 Kings 5:15–16). A gratitude not for Elisha but for what God did through Elisha. His life is changed forever from that moment.

But perhaps like with Naaman, God is speaking through our situation in a strange way or through someone we might discount. Will we listen? Will we obey? Even when it doesn't make sense?

The miracle awaits. And maybe it's in the form of strange obedience. But obedience to God is something we'll never regret.

TAKE THIS DEVOTION DEEPER

Read all of 2 Kings 5.

What are qualities you should look for in others before you take their advice?

What is an example of instruction or wisdom God has given you before through another person?

15

Believe That What God Ordains, He Sustains

But the eye of their God was on the elders of the Jews, and they did not stop them until the report should reach Darius and then an answer be returned by letter concerning it.

Ezra 5:5

Discouragement is something we all deal with, and at some point, a decision must be made to believe this:

> WHAT GOD ORDAINS, HE SUSTAINS.

Discouragement is in the emotional atmosphere for the Jews as we open Ezra 5 today because naysayers have entered their stories.

God said to build the temple (Ezra 1:2–3). So, it's settled. It has to be done. No matter how long it takes. And with or without whoever is—or isn't—part of the process.

God ordained it

But the people were discouraged and frustrated. I imagine they wrestled with thinking, *Is this really going to happen?*

And now that the rebuilding had begun, oh yes, the naysayers had arrived, and they were asking questions (Ezra 5:3–5).

Anytime we start to fulfill the things God has called us to, we have to say no to the naysayers, because they will be there.

This is why Ezra 5:5 is something for us to hold on to: "But the eye of their God was on the elders of the Jews . . ."

When God's eye is on something, we do not have to worry if someone is critical or negative about what we're doing. Because . . .

When we are doing God's work, He is with us (Joshua 1:9).

When we are doing God's work, He is for us (Zephaniah 3:17).

When we are doing God's work, His favor is on us (Psalm 5:12).

God sustained it

This is the message Haggai and Zechariah desperately tried to help the Jews understand—that despite the time, the energy, and the efforts that seemed to be returning void, they were not void. They needed the people to know that their prophecies were not wishful thinking but truly biblical hope.

They encouraged the building project to get going again, and it did, but their encouragement was met with more resistance, more questions, and more doubt (Ezra 5:1–6).

So, they went straight to the top. A letter was sent to King Darius (Ezra 5:7–17).

Tattenai, a governor, sent a letter asking King Darius to search for the original rebuilding decree issued by Cyrus (Ezra 5:17). The truth needed to be found.

In the same way, when the voice of the naysayer comes, whether in person or in our mind, we have to search out Truth ourselves. The Holy Spirit helps us seek out Truth today, in a letter as well—in Scripture (Jeremiah 29:13).

Scripture takes us straight to the top, to the heart of God (Philippians 4:6–7).

Each time we filter our discouragement from naysayers through biblical hope, we build holy confidence that we have a God who is who He says He is.

So, if He said it, He'll do it. If He says we have it, we have it. And if He says it's possible, it is. The eye of our God is on you as you do His work on this earth. So, we can confidently say *no* to the naysayers and *yes* to God's Truth.

But ultimately, the decision is ours to make.

Decide to believe this with me today: what God ordains, God sustains.

TAKE THIS DEVOTION DEEPER

Read all of Ezra 5 and look up and read each of the verses listed in this devotion.

Write down anything you feel like you are struggling to believe God ordained and will ultimately sustain:

16

Stay on the Road toward Righteousness and Wisdom

In the path of righteousness is life, and in its pathway there is no death.

Proverbs 12:28

There's a saying: "You have to go down a lot of wrong roads to find the right one."

I don't know how true that is, but I've taken a lot of wrong roads physically, spiritually, and emotionally. My guess is that all of us can relate to wrong-road realities—those moments, days, or even months we find ourselves in the complete opposite place of where we wanted to be. One wrong decision leads to the next, and we find ourselves wondering, *How did I get here?*

The book of Proverbs is a continuous invitation to walk the road that leads us to wisdom. This path helps transform our thoughts, words, and actions into godly wisdom. But the decision to do so is ours.

We'll always be tempted to veer off on the wrong road because we're human. But as we study Proverbs and apply this wisdom to our lives, it brings much more understanding of how to stay on the road less traveled, the road of righteousness.

Throughout Proverbs 12, there's a frequent pairing of two words: *righteous* and *wicked* (Proverbs 12:3, 5, 7, 12, 21).

Righteousness is the process of learning to think, speak, and act with godly wisdom. We live righteously when we live by faith (Romans 1:17), quickly admit our wrongs (James 5:16; 1 John 1:9), and study Scripture intently (2 Timothy 3:16).

The opposite of righteous is *wrong*, *evil*, or *wicked*. We step onto this road when we decide to do things our own way, without God (2 John 1:9).

Because these two words, *righteous* and *wicked*, are used repeatedly throughout this text, it's important for us to lean in and listen to what King Solomon is communicating.

In Proverbs 12, so much of King Solomon's wisdom about pursuing righteousness points to our words.

> ## WHEN HIS WORDS HELP OUR WORDS, THEY BECOME RIGHTEOUS, OR WE COULD SAY, KEEP US ON THE RIGHT ROAD.

Here are a few of the words of wisdom he passes along to help us in our decision-making processes to stay on the road toward righteousness.

Wise thoughts are a vital part of the road to righteousness (Proverbs 12:5)

What if we started each day asking God to guide our thoughts on the path of righteousness? (Psalm 119:15). A simple prayer like, "God, please don't let me think anything about myself, others, or situations today that don't line up with Your Truth." I have seen how taking the time to set my mind in the right direction each day really helps me stay on the righteous path. Because our thoughts eventually become our words.

Wise words are fruitful and full of good things on the road to righteousness (Proverbs 12:14)

What was the last thing you said? Was it fruitful? Good? Wise? In our culture, so much attention is given to being a great listener in conversation, but let's also pay close attention to the fruit we're leaving in a conversation once we open our mouths to speak. We can lead others to the path of righteousness with the things we say (Daniel 12:3).

Wise words should be surrounded by truth, not lies, on the road to righteousness (Proverbs 12:17, 19, 22)

It's so easy to slip out a little white lie or even participate in gossip. But the more we surround ourselves with Truth and godly wisdom in our thoughts and in our conversations, the more likely we'll steer off those wrong-word roads that can lead to destruction (Ephesians 4:25; Psalm 15:2).

Because of wisdom like today's reading, we can steer our thoughts and words onto the road of righteousness. And, when we find ourselves on the wrong road, we can remember these truths and ask God to help us (again) to walk in wisdom.

It's never too early or too late in our lives to make the decision to move onto the right road. God always meets us where we are, not where we wish we were.

TAKE THIS DEVOTION DEEPER

Read all of Proverbs 12. In your Bible, highlight any of the key verses you sense the Holy Spirit asking you to pay attention to. Revisit the verses throughout the day, and ask the Holy Spirit to turn your attention to what your soul needs most today.

17

MAKE THE DECISION TO

Step Out of the Shadows and Into the Light

Rejoice not over me, O my enemy; when I fall, I shall rise; when I sit in darkness, the LORD will be a light to me.

Micah 7:8

Each of us has something inside us emotionally that's called *shadow beliefs.*

It's a psychological concept that ties back to our childhood, and in these shadows of our souls are some negative beliefs that fuel our inner critic based on childhood experiences.

These beliefs tell us things like . . .

- *You will never succeed at this*
- *You are not equipped for this*
- *Give up, it's over*
- *Don't even bother trying*

Not long ago, I felt like I failed at something important to me. And mercy, that inner critic was loud. Those shadows got really big.

A shadow is the place of darkness in the midst of light. It's a place where things can be hidden from the light. And shadows are not the place we need to hang out.

The Bible reminds us in Micah 7:8 that when we are surrounded by darkness, we can make a decision to believe this:

IN GOD, THERE IS NO DARKNESS AND NO SHADOWS.

But what do we do in our heads after this moment of realization? That's where the real decision of choosing light or darkness in our souls is made.

Notice in Micah 7:8 the text says "when I sit in darkness."

Despite our past and the story of failure that shadow beliefs want us to believe, we have to step out of the shadow and into the Light. This is where God can change the way we have allowed our inner critic to define us.

I felt like I failed. But I learned some powerful lessons because I stepped out of the shadow beliefs in my head and into the Light.

Listen, you don't have time for that shadow mess. Decide right now to get out of the shadow and into the Light. Yes, there are some lessons to learn from our failures, but they will not define our future.

TAKE THIS DEVOTION DEEPER

What is the darkness that you feel surrounds you today?

Read Psalm 37:24. What does this verse say upholds you when you fall?

What is one shadow belief you have? Write it below:

Pray and ask God to give you the wisdom to help bring light to this dark place.

18

Soar Today

But those who trust in the Lord will find new strength. They will soar high on wings like eagles. They will run and not grow weary. They will walk and not faint.

Isaiah 40:31 NLT

There are some seasons of life that leave us feeling like we're falling more than flying.

Losing my mom, my only brother, my last living grandparent, and our family horse in a two-year span definitely left a lingering feeling that I was falling again and again.

All of it didn't seem fair. Didn't seem believable. Didn't seem like so much loss could happen in such a short time. And rightly so, it left me feeling like the next loss was always just around the corner.

I felt stuck in discouragement and doom, like it was impossible to get up from all the feelings of defeat I was wrestling with.

My guess is you too have had a season, whether long or short, that's made you feel like it was going to be difficult to get back up.

Sometimes we wonder if our grief, disappointments, or failures have pushed us to the point of no return. This is why Isaiah 40:31 has become my anchor for the days ahead.

Reading it in the context of the entire chapter of Isaiah 40, verse 31 (NLT) is truly where we see the power and promise: "But those who trust in the LORD will find new strength. They will soar high on wings like eagles. They will run and not grow weary. They will walk and not faint."

In this chapter, Isaiah is speaking to people who are in extreme distress for a variety of reasons. Seasons of falling bring these distress-filled feelings front and center.

Throughout this entire chapter, Isaiah reminds his listeners that God is in charge of everything. But he also challenges them to wrestle with their doubt, sin, fear, and questions.

Hard seasons bring questions.

> **BUT JUST BECAUSE WE HAVE QUESTIONS DOESN'T NECESSARILY MEAN WE'RE QUESTIONING GOD.**

After reading this chapter in a sobering posture of the reality of life, I arrived at verse 31. Through Isaiah's words, I'm reminded that our God is very real, incredibly strong, and bigger than anything seasons of distress can bring.

He creates a way for us to go up higher, or as this verse says, "soar," in the midst of it all.

How?

By waiting in trust for God to strengthen us through our sorrow.

But this isn't necessarily a sitting-still motion. It's a space where we decide to fill our time with worship instead of worry. It's when we decide to simply pray His promises when our words are hard to find in prayer. And it's when we decide to replace our distress-filled doubt with the reality of who our God is.

All of these decisions can help us get up when the trials of this weary world try to keep us down. And one day, we'll be able to look back on our seasons of falling and see the God who helped us get back up, again and again.

Each day, when my heart starts to ache over the loss I've experienced, I pull out Isaiah 40:31 and decide to let this promise from God help me back up and soar again.

God will do the same for you. Wait in trust. Worship through the worry. Remember who your God is. And find yourself experiencing a strength to carry on that can only come from heaven's throne.

TAKE THIS DEVOTION DEEPER

Using the acronym below for SOAR, look up each of the verses connected to the word to help you soar today.

S Surrender—Jeremiah 10:23

O Obey—James 1:22

A Ask—Matthew 26:39

R Rest—Matthew 11:28

19

MAKE THE DECISION TO
Lean In and Listen to Wisdom and Warning

Should this be said, O house of Jacob? Has the LORD grown impatient? Are these his deeds? Do not my words do good to him who walks uprightly?

Micah 2:7

When my middle daughter was about five years old, we went through this trying phase with her. Beyond typical temper tantrums and silly childhood tactics, she started saying one phrase every time she did something we asked her not to do: "But, I didn't know!"

The problem was, she definitely knew. And frequently, she had been warned not to do said activity. This response made me a lot less sympathetic toward her misbehavior. You expect more from your kids once they are able to understand directions and warnings.

Micah 2 has a similar theme of false naïveness. I am imagining the people Micah is preaching to and giving warning to voicing something so similar: "We didn't know!"

But, they did know. They had received these warnings before. And they still chose to disregard the directions and warnings God had given them (Micah 2:6–9).

In the two opening verses of chapter 2, Micah says that not only are evil things happening but also people are intentionally doing evil things (Micah 2:1–2).

Sin will always be sin, and we will always struggle with it. But there is a hope God has for us, that we would continue to grow as we continue to know. Just knowing or hearing won't change our lives.

In verses 6 and 11, Micah describes a prophet the people wanted to hear from. They didn't want to hear warnings. But Micah, like all the minor prophets we've been studying, reminds us that God's message isn't always the popular one.

I wonder, if someone like Micah was out and about declaring these things in our modern world, who would receive it?

In our world today, we can have a very lopsided perception of people who give warnings. I tend to envision someone angry, standing on a street corner and holding a sign that says, "Repent or Die!"

And while that type of message delivery doesn't spread very far, sometimes I wonder if God puts people close to me to reveal His merciful mystery through a simple moment of conviction.

It could be a friend giving us "that look" when we say something we shouldn't.

Possibly our kids or spouse telling us we offended them.

Or maybe a boss giving feedback about the time we might be wasting.

None of us are exempt from the need for spiritual growth.

> ## WHEN WE RESIST THIS PLACE WHERE GOD IS TRYING TO REVEAL OPPORTUNITIES FOR GROWTH, WE CAN END UP LIVING IN DENIAL-FILLED SITUATIONS THAT MAY BRING UNWANTED RESULTS.

No, this isn't the feel-good message of our faith.

We didn't know? Or, we didn't listen?

Pride would love for us to plead ignorance to our sin struggle instead of taking intentional steps each day to see what we need to see, change what we need to change, and stay humble enough to receive caution from other people.

And while this message can feel heavy and unwanted, Micah is also a hopeful prophet.

Verses 12 and 13 of this chapter reveal the power of restoration that could come. Today we have the Spirit, a Counselor and a Helper, to lead us as we continue to know and grow (Galatians 5:25).

We can make the decision to lean in and listen to wisdom and warnings in God's Word. It's a process of strengthening. One that will help us become a little stronger in our weakest places.

TAKE THIS DEVOTION DEEPER

After reading Micah 2, what is your takeaway from this chapter?

What are some warnings from the Bible you wish others would listen to? How can you gently lead others to follow the instructions God gives us?

20

Be Emotionally Generous
toward Others

Give, and it will be given to you. A good measure, pressed down, shaken
together and running over, will be poured into your lap. For with the
measure you use, it will be measured to you.

Luke 6:38 NIV

We were out of milk, so I headed to the store with my party
of five.

Even though we were in a time crunch, I wanted to make
the most of our trip and pick up a few other things. Our family divided up—
my husband went to the row of toilet paper, our oldest daughter walked off
to get bread, our middle daughter headed out for fruit, and the youngest
one, Kennedy Grace, trekked to the milk fridge with me.

Everyone quickly got what they needed and met back at the register—
except my husband. At the self-checkout with my three girls, I scanned our
items, thinking Kris would be there any second. But he wasn't. As the line

behind me quickly grew long and impatient, I wondered if I should cancel my order and step out of line.

But time was short, and we were already running late. So in this unnerving moment, I instructed my youngest daughter to run and get the toilet paper from her daddy. She took off, found my husband, and secured the rolls under her arm. But, on her way back to the self-checkout, a sparkly cereal display distracted her.

In a calm yet firm voice, I made sure my daughter heard me. "Kennedy Grace, come here right now, please."

Now, she figured the fastest way to get that toilet paper to me was to slide it down the aisle. Without hesitation, she whooshed the package right to me.

The people standing behind me thought my daughter's idea was quite amusing. Everyone except one woman.

As Kennedy Grace giggled, jumped, and bounced her way to the register, I knew this wasn't the time or place to have a teachable moment, so I just muttered quietly for her to calm down.

That one woman, feeling it was a good time to teach my daughter a lesson, said to me, "Well, isn't she something?"

I didn't want to get into a hot confrontational mess, so I ignored her and bagged my items.

But then she asked Kennedy Grace, "Why are you acting up so much?"
Kennedy replied, "I'm just tired."

And then the woman responded with a statement no stressed-out momma needs to hear: "Well maybe your mom should put you to bed earlier."

What did she just say? Uh-uh. I gulped and took a deep breath, ready to blurt out something sassy. But in the midst of this chaos, in the midst of this tension, I felt the presence of God hold me back with this thought: *Give her what you need most.*

I needed to give this woman a piece of my mind, is what my soul screamed.

But it was true. I need a lot of grace these days. Grace. Grace. Grace.

So, I said nothing. I extended grace. I smiled, grabbed Kennedy's hand, and walked out of the grocery store, challenged by the thought of Luke 6:38: "Give, and it will be given to you. A good measure, pressed down, shaken together and running over, will be poured into your lap. For with the measure you use, it will be measured to you."

I make a lot of mistakes. I forget about important things. And I too have judged stressed-out mommas in the grocery store with misbehaving children. But Scripture tells us that when we give to others what we need, something very freeing happens: we receive what we need, too.

> **WHEN WE MAKE THE DECISION TO BE EMOTIONALLY GENEROUS TO OTHERS, WE CREATE THE ATMOSPHERE FOR GOD TO DO SOMETHING POWERFUL IN US AND THROUGH US.**

I don't always want to give others what I need. My initial reaction is often to give others what I think they deserve.

A quick comeback.

A nasty look.

An unforgiving heart.

But none of these things has ever brought me anything I needed.

As I continue to live out this verse in Luke, I'm focusing on others' needs and reacting based on them, not myself.

But the next time we needed milk, I also made *another* decision: I went to the grocery store *alone*.

TAKE THIS DEVOTION DEEPER

What is something you need in your life right now?

How can you give that to someone else today?

21

Accept What Is for Today and Hold On to Hope for Tomorrow

Hope deferred makes the heart sick, but a desire fulfilled is a tree of life.

Proverbs 13:12

I once heard someone say, "You are fully healed when you have no desire to look back on what didn't happen."

Recently, I remembered this quote as I was going through an old journal, looking at several goals, dreams, and hopes I had written down over the last five years.

One by one, several things were crossed off the list; they didn't happen and weren't going to happen. Why? Because of death, broken relationships, unmet career goals, circumstances, and in some cases just the way things played out.

The problem was, I kept replaying these disappointing events like a reel in my mind.

Wondering things like, *If I had taken this certain step, would the outcome have changed?*

Or, *If I had made that specific move, would it have prevented this unwanted reality?*

And, *If I had spoken up about this or that, would anything be different today?*

Maybe some people would say this is living in a place of regret. But to me, when I recalled the quote about looking back on what didn't happen, I realized what this thought process really was.

Unmet hope for the past. And I couldn't stop looking at it.

If I'm honest, I'd been viewing the pain of my unmet hopes through the wrong spiritual lens. My soul felt sick from past disappointments, and I thought if I accepted the disappointments, I was losing hope.

Something inside me longed for God Himself to rewrite the past and make right all those unmet hopes. I wanted my Lazarus moment (John 11), a miraculous resurrection of all those things on my list.

I didn't know what to do with my many feelings about my unmet hopes until I began to study today's key verse, Proverbs 13:12: "Hope deferred makes the heart sick, but a desire fulfilled is a tree of life."

Proverbs is a book of wisdom. Chapter 13 is full of practical steps for living a godly life. Some Bible scholars believe verse 12 refers to the longing we have for heaven, where all our unmet hopes will be no more. And the Hebrew word for *hope* here in this verse means "expectation."

God cares deeply about the hopes and the longings we have. Even the smallest ones (1 Peter 5:7; Luke 12:7). But God doesn't promise us every expectation we have here on this earth will be fulfilled the way we see fit. Things will happen in our life that will lead to disappointment.

Maybe you are thinking of something today that to you feels unfair, wrong, hurtful, or like an unmet hope or expectation.

Though our disappointments may be different, I bet we would find a common ground in that we tend to put emotional Band-Aids on those unmet hopes. And the peeling off of those Band-Aids is painful to even think about.

Yet the emotional wounds remain. And they often begin to show in the most unlikely ways.

The tears that seem to appear out of nowhere, the lack of desire to pray, the eye rolls when someone else complains about something they have that we have hoped for.

When we accept that the past didn't go the way we hoped or dreamed, it's not a failure. It's actually one of the healthiest things we can do for our souls. It releases us to start looking ahead and get our hopes up again for all the goodness God still has for our lives.

I've learned the first step to healing the emotional wound of unmet hopes is to make the decision to accept what is. The second step is to ask God to help us stop looking back and instead look ahead with a holy expectation. And we may need to repeat that process again and again.

> GOD PROBABLY ISN'T GOING TO REWRITE OUR PAST, BUT HE PROMISES HE ALREADY HAS AN AMAZING FUTURE WRITTEN FOR US THAT WILL BE FULFILLED.

May our unmet hopes of yesterday stop holding captive our thoughts . . . so we can confidently look forward to the hopes that are still to come.

TAKE THIS DEVOTION DEEPER

Look up and read the following verses:

Jeremiah 29:11
Philippians 1:6
Romans 15:13

What is something in your life you need to stop replaying from the past?

Write out a prayer and ask God to give you a holy expectation for your future:

22

MAKE THE DECISION TO
Seek Wisdom in the Word of God

Take away the dross from the silver, and the smith has material for a vessel.

Proverbs 25:4

Sometimes the problems around me can distract me from being wise. I get caught up in the details, the issue, the stress, and trying to find a solution to a problem rather than the perspective of wisdom a problem offers. Every problem offers us the opportunity to seek and search for wisdom.

Proverbs guides us through this process of searching out wisdom. It gives us the ultimate picture of what it looks like to be a wise vessel for God.

In chapter 25, we come across a word used to describe something as worthless, rubbish, trash. "Take away the dross from the silver, and the smith has material for a vessel" (Proverbs 25:4). Dross is a substance that is removed during the purification process to make silver. Basically, it's just . . . yuck.

Wouldn't you agree we all have some soul dross keeping us from being wise vessels? It's what tends to happen naturally when a problem appears for me. The dross looks like:

Harshness
Not thinking the best of others or the situation
Stress
Anxiety

This soul dross can keep me from making wise decisions in the midst of a problem or conflict. But if we want the best in our lives, the dross has to come out.

> **EVERY FORM OF DROSS IN OUR SOULS CAN FIND A THREAD OF PRIDE ATTACHED TO IT. BUT BECAUSE OF THE STRENGTH WE FIND IN JESUS, THAT THREAD OF PRIDE CAN ALSO BE DETACHED.**

We can take a look at the kings we find in the Bible to confirm this. The best kings were full of humility. The worst? Full of pride.

King Hezekiah was one of the best. Thanks to him, we have this record of how to search for wisdom. He collected the teachings in Proverbs 25–29 from Solomon during his rule in Judah.

Why is this important to know as we study?

Proverbs 25:2 tells us, "It is the glory of God to conceal things, but the glory of kings is to search things out."

Good kings had to learn to ask the right questions, see things from a different perspective, and make decisions for their people based on wisdom.

Hezekiah was a good, wise king because he listened and sought out wisdom from wise people (2 Kings 18:3). He did not arrogantly think he could figure things out on his own. He sought out the answers. His posture of humility was one of the keys to his success.

As we long for wisdom in our lives, we would do well to remember the process Hezekiah walked through. We may not be a king, but we have problems. Conflicts and tragedies will come our way.

But the next time a problem pops up in our lives, may we remember Solomon, Hezekiah, and the many others in the Bible and the wisdom they have left us. It's our decision to open the Word of God and seek it out.

TAKE THIS DEVOTION DEEPER

What is something you need wisdom for in your life today?

What are some verses that come to mind about this struggle?

Who is someone in the Bible you could study closer who may have struggled with this same issue?

23

Stay in a Posture of Repentance toward God

For the LORD is restoring the majesty of Jacob as the majesty of Israel,
for plunderers have plundered them and ruined their branches.

Nahum 2:2

I'm not sure I've ever sat down to read the Bible and thought, *Let me turn to the book of Nahum for some encouragement today.* This is a very unfamiliar book of the Bible to most people. But it is filled with wisdom we need to hear.

It's hard to read about God's warnings of consequences, and that's what this book is full of.

> **OUR SOULS SEEM TO CRAVE THE THINGS THAT MAKE US BETTER HUMAN BEINGS BUT RESIST THE THINGS THAT MAKE US UNCOMFORTABLE.**

And the more I read chapter 2 of Nahum, the more I'm a little overwhelmed at how discouraging it can be to read chapters in the Bible where warnings turn into reality.

Judgment has come for Nineveh. A hundred and fifty years before this moment, Jonah, the prophet, was preaching that judgment would come.

And Nahum is preparing the people for what's just ahead. He sees it, and there's no turning back now. But hope is still tucked away in this battle of darkness. In verse 2, Nahum reminds us that even though all these bad things are unfolding, God is restoring the majesty of Jacob and Israel.

And as we look at our current reality, what does God want to restore in us? What are the warnings we aren't listening to? And what do we see coming?

There are two things we can see from this verse that will help us make the decision to stay repentant toward God:

1. God will always receive a heart of repentance

Recently, I was on an airplane with a man who was questioning the Bible. And he said, "So let me get this straight. You believe that a person can live an awful life, do horrible things, and on his deathbed, he can repent and God will forgive him?" I took a deep breath, understanding all too well his question, and said, "Yes. This is the character of our God. He forgives. Even at the last moment. It doesn't mean we won't be judged, but He will always forgive." The thief on the cross next to Jesus is a perfect example of this (Luke 23:39–43).

But Nahum is describing what is about to happen to Nineveh. Because even though they did repent, as we saw in the book of Jonah, they turned back to their sinful ways.

They abandoned their revival.

And each day God offers us a place of personal revival through the presence of the Holy Spirit. But it's up to us to step into that place, where sometimes it does, in fact, feel a little uncomfortable.

It doesn't matter how many times it takes us to get it; God will always forgive.

2. God will not be mocked

This sin struggle is nothing new. Nahum is preaching the same message Jonah preached about one hundred fifty years prior (Jonah 3).

The bad news? Some of us, like Nahum, see what's coming. It's right in front of us. For us personally and for us globally.

In our own lives, when we are convicted of sin, we have to remember that God is offering us a personal revival. He's able to restore all the enemy has taken from us. Only we have to choose to repent of our sins in order to receive this revival.

Revival always begins with repentance.

It's not easy or comfortable to study things like this. But when we look at the Bible as a whole, not just pick out the parts we like or don't like, we get to see the whole picture of God's character and plan for our world.

Nineveh didn't repent and therefore received God's consequences. But we can be wiser and make decisions today that lead us toward a posture of repentance before God.

TAKE THIS DEVOTION DEEPER

Write down something you feel convicted by the Holy Spirit to repent from today:

Pray and ask for forgiveness and take a minute to learn anything you need to from this important time with God. This is truly one of the ways we become wiser.

Read Matthew 3:8. How does repentance help produce fruit in our lives?

24

MAKE THE DECISION TO
Choose to Fight for Faith

When I am afraid, I put my trust in you.

Psalm 56:3

The doorbell rang at 1:00 a.m. Instantly, I knew something was wrong. Panic rose in my body as I fumbled to find my glasses and get to the door.

There stood my friend with a look of worry and a command to hurry.

I grabbed my keys and drove as quickly as I could to the hospital, where someone I deeply love was in an emergency room bed. Choices they'd made led to bad decisions and an outcome that almost cost them their life.

They would be OK. They would pull through. They would wake up again. But the next few hours—and even the next few days—were going to be hard.

There were two unseen things fighting for my attention in those moments. One was faith. The other was fear. But the battle to believe one or the other would be mine.

Having fear is not a sin. It's what we allow fear to become that leads us to turn away from God. In fact, throughout Scripture, we see how God fights for our faith in the midst of our fears. As King David wrote in today's key verse, Psalm 56:3, God longs for us to trust Him: "When I am afraid, I put my trust in you."

I love this verse because it's not just a promise I can hold on to but a prayer I can pray when I feel afraid. This verse is a verse of resolve when fear fights for our focus.

But is it as simple as praying a prayer and asking God to help us have faith instead of fear? Yes and no.

> ## WE CAN SILENCE FEAR BY GIVING STEADY FOCUS TO FAITH.

And so, over the next few hours in that hospital room and when we left the hospital, I had to give my faith the attention it needed in a crisis. I repeatedly had to remind my thoughts not to give way to fear. And I know God heard my prayer: "I'm afraid . . . but I'm putting my trust in You."

I don't know what's fighting for your attention that stirs up fear in your life, but I hope you find the confidence to break through the unseen and hold on to faith. Because God is fighting for you, too. Start with this prayer: "I'm afraid . . . but I'm putting my trust in You." And then recognize the process.

You're worthy of faith. And fear isn't worthy of your attention.

Faith and fear both fight for you to believe in something you cannot see. Becoming wiser with the Lord means we step into this battleground and speak faith. The decision is ours; choose your battle wisely.

TAKE THIS DEVOTION DEEPER

Read all of Psalm 56 in your Bible. Highlight or underline other verses in this passage that stand out to you to help you build your faith. Share one of those verses with someone you care about today.

25

Become the Most Authentic Version Possible of You

And I am sure of this, that he who began a good work in you will bring it to completion at the day of Jesus Christ.

Philippians 1:6

The bathroom mirror seems to be the culprit of these types of conversations within me. I stand there day after day, bushing hair, examining wrinkles and blemishes, looking into my tired, worn-out eyes while wondering . . . *Who are you really becoming?*

The truth is, these days I've let too much noise in. Understanding who I am becoming feels hard to determine. I feel stuck, like there's a *me* trying to get out, but I find myself living in the leftovers of so many life situations.

I guess I always assumed that by this point in my life, I would know exactly who I was and where I was going. But as Paul reminds us in Philippians 1:6, our process of growing in Christ toward a place of authenticity is one we will continually work through. Until we take our last breath or

Jesus returns, there's a need to make the decision to become the most authentic version of ourselves each day.

And so, as I try to *unstick* my life process today, I'm thinking through what it really means to become *me.*

I'm giving myself these permissions, these orders, these *Five Authenticity Declarations* so to speak . . . to help me stay true to myself while becoming myself. Maybe if you are feeling a little lost today they will speak to you, too.

1. You shall live as though life is a process of becoming

This process of discovering who we really are isn't something we simply awaken to one day. Life's peaks, valleys, and plateaus all lead us through this process. While life has a start line and a finish line, much of the in-between isn't so definable. But each day has something to offer in the shaping of our souls.

2. You shall pay close attention to the people you are surrounding yourself with

That saying, "You become most like the five people you spend the most amount of time with," is true. Do you leave the company of those five people feeling inspired and better about yourself or anxious and fearful of everything you said? Choose your five wisely.

3. You shall embrace where you are, not where you wish to be

Life is short. Assume today is all you get. We cannot really live by chasing the "One day . . ." scenarios. What if this is it? As we embrace our *now* in life, it will help us live life each day and not feel like we're always waiting on what's next.

4. You shall have permission to change your mind

That color you thought you would love until the grave and now you hate? It's OK to change your mind. That job you worked so hard to get but now you are just not sure? It's OK to change your mind. Living as you is messy and complicated. It's OK to change your mind, even more than once.

5. You shall do something each day that makes you feel alive

We will lose ourselves faster when we stay in the cycle of busy and go. What is it that makes you feel alive? Is it snapping a picture? Feeling dirt beneath your feet? Watching the sunset or sunrise? Is it laughing until your core hurts? Press pause on busy and make an effort each day toward those things that make you feel alive.

Becoming wiser means we make the decision to become the most authentic version of ourselves possible. It means we decide to love who God created us to be while always striving to be more like Jesus.

TAKE THIS DEVOTION DEEPER

Which of these declarations do you need the most today?

Write a prayer out and ask God to help you keep becoming the most authentic and true version of who He created you to be:

26

Fight Off Isolation

The LORD God said, "It is not good for the man to be alone."
Genesis 2:18 NIV

I'm in the midst of a challenging project for my career. And maybe challenging projects are exciting to you, but what it really means for me is sitting for hours on end in sweatpants staring at a blinking cursor. Reading documents aloud to your dog starts to feel normal. And cereal accounts for dinner at least two nights a week.

This project is my dream. I feel like I've been waiting for this opportunity for a lifetime. So, I feel bad for the next words I'm about to say. But this dream feels incredibly . . . lonely.

Most days, it's just me and my thoughts for hours and hours. Sometimes I'll email a few thoughts to a friend and ask her honest opinion, but 90 percent of the time, it's just me and my thoughts.

And when that's the company you keep for days, your thoughts can mess with you:

You can't really do this.
They picked the wrong woman for this project.

Deadlines and other demands have made it almost impossible to incorporate time with friends in this season. But as I've talked with other women, it seems I'm not alone in my loneliness struggle.

I hear women all the time say, "I feel so . . . isolated."

For some, it has to do with hectic schedules—there's no time for friendships. Others have been deeply wounded by people—there's no desire for community. And many, like me, are in a different season of life than others in their circle of friends.

But the other day, a friend unexpectedly stopped by to pick up something. A family member opened the door, while I was in sweatpants, hadn't had a shower, and really just wanted to sit in my office and work. But I knew my friend would think it very rude if I didn't at least say hello.

So I took a deep breath, excused my appearance (which thankfully she cared nothing about), and we ended up in an hour-long conversation. We didn't talk about work or deadlines . . . we just shared about our lives.

And it was the most refreshing hour I'd had in a long time. I left that conversation with the confidence to get back into my working rhythm.

As I read Genesis 2:18 (NIV), I was reminded how from the very beginning, God designed us to be in relationship with others: "Then the LORD God said, 'It is not good for the man to be alone.'"

Although this verse refers to the creation of Adam and Eve, the first man and woman, it's clear God created us with a longing, a need, to have people speak into our lives.

It's so easy for us to forget this. Or let our pride convince us we don't need people in our corner.

> **ISOLATION'S BIGGEST LIE IS THAT WE SOMEHOW CAN THRIVE THROUGH LIFE WITHOUT SOMEONE BY OUR SIDE.**

But one of the wisest things we can do to grow ourselves and our faith is to make the decision to fight off isolation. Make the decision to surround yourself with community. Connect with at least one person. Say yes to the invite. And be someone who also extends invites.

TAKE THIS DEVOTION DEEPER

Read Ecclesiastes 4:9–12. Write down the benefits listed of having someone alongside you.

Who is someone you can invite into your life today? Make a decision now to reach out to them at some point today.

27

MAKE THE DECISION TO

Follow One Instruction You Know God Has Given You Today

Remember this also in my favor, O my God, and spare me according to the greatness of your steadfast love.

Nehemiah 13:22

Growing up, I was a latchkey kid. This meant I was normally met after school by a note on the counter with instructions for the afternoon, signed: *Love, Mom*. Sometimes I got distracted or just didn't feel like doing what my mom asked me to do. Obviously, she wasn't super happy about this when she got home.

> IT'S EASY TO DO WHAT WE'RE SUPPOSED TO DO WHEN SOMEONE IS WATCHING, LEADING, AND GUIDING US, BUT WHAT ABOUT WHEN WE'RE LEFT TO OUR OWN DEVICES?

There's a man in the Bible who has many lessons to teach about leadership. His name is Nehemiah. One of Nehemiah's greatest wins as a leader was the fact that he helped rebuild the wall around Jerusalem.

After the celebration of the rebuilding of the wall, Nehemiah traveled from Jerusalem to Persia (Nehemiah 13:6). Some Bible scholars believe it would have been about a one-hundred-day journey there and back, but how long Nehemiah stayed in Persia isn't known. What is known is that when he returned, things were not how they were supposed to be.

There were a few layers to the things Nehemiah was upset about. Laws, covenants, and oaths were being broken. The Levites had been wronged (Nehemiah 13:10). The Sabbath had been broken (Nehemiah 13:15–22). But the biggest issue was that Eliashib, the current priest, allowed Tobiah, the enemy (Nehemiah 2:10; 4:7–8), to move in to one of the most important rooms of the temple (Nehemiah 13:5).

I imagine Nehemiah was discouraged and disappointed that his absence of leadership led to all this chaos. And he had a very strong reaction and violent response toward the people (Nehemiah 13:25).

Nehemiah closes out chapter 13 with a very sober, simple statement: "Remember me, O my God, for good" (Nehemiah 13:31). This wasn't a plea for glory. Maybe these words flowed from worry. Was what he witnessed among the Israelites a reflection of his leadership?

The answer is no.

Because since the beginning of time, humans have been doing things their own way when they thought no one would know.

Nothing we will ever do could change the leadership God has over our lives. But it's up to us to decide what we'll do with the instruction, wisdom, and guidance that's been given to us in Scripture. May we make the decision today to follow the command we know God has given us.

And when we stumble or stray, may we remember that we have the greatest note of instruction left for us on the cross. And with the kindest ending: *Love, God*.

TAKE THIS DEVOTION DEEPER

Read all of Nehemiah 13.

What is something in your relationship with God where you seem to keep stumbling?

Pray and ask God for wisdom in that area, and write down what you sense the Lord is leading you to do:

28

MAKE THE DECISION TO

Expect That Today Can Be Different

> For I am about to do something new. See, I have already begun! Do you not see it? I will make a pathway through the wilderness. I will create rivers in the dry wasteland.
>
> Isaiah 43:19 NLT

I t's the same stupid fight with my husband again and again. You were supposed to stop by the store; I was supposed to pick this kid up.

It's the redundant load of laundry again and again. The missing socks, the torn jeans, and the mud-stained shirt.

It's the predictable drive to and from work again and again. Wait for the light to turn green, pause for the train, and make that last phone call of the day.

It's the expected social media feed. I'm mad at the government, no one likes me, see where I am and you're not.

Dear life, you can wear a girl's passion down.

But then that same girl lays her head on her pillow; she drifts off to sleep, dreaming of being in another place, in another season. The moon drifts over her house. And then the sun peeks through her blinds at a very early hour.

And something new is stirred within her: Isaiah 43:19.

Sometimes life needs a new rhythm.

"For I am about to do something new . . ."

Sometimes routines need to be rejuvenated.

"See, I have already begun . . ."

Sometimes spreading ourselves so thin makes it impossible to fully involve ourselves with the things we once loved.

"Do you not see it?"

When we find ourselves in the ruts of the wilderness, we need a different path. And some days we need to just wake up and make a conscious decision that today is the day something is going to be different.

Because we forget the power of the gospel message, how following Jesus isn't meant to just make us feel better. It's a path of continual renewal.

And when life's paths become passionless, often we replace theology with various forms of unbiblical therapy.

Retail therapy. Vitamin D therapy. Friend therapy. Project therapy. Food therapy.

The world offers us a slew of paths to make our lives more fulfilling. But at the end of each of those paths is the same result: more wilderness.

But we, as followers of Jesus, are not looking for the same path everyone else travels down.

> **WE ARE LOOKING FOR A NEW WAY IN THE MIDST OF NORMALNESS. WE NEED A PATH THAT LEADS FROM FAITH TO FAITH.**

"I will make a pathway through the wilderness . . ."

On the path of faith to faith, we can find God in the mundane, everyday moments of life.

"I will create rivers in the dry wasteland . . ."

So today, I'm making a decision to seek the newness this day offers. It allows me to find hope in the expectation of the possibility that today can be different.

Today can be the day of new beginnings.

Today can be the day of renewal.

Today can be the day of an increased presence of God in our lives.

Today can be the day we just decide it's going to be different.

TAKE THIS DEVOTION DEEPER

Isaiah 43:19 is connected to Numbers 20:11—read this verse. What came out of the rock?

How would this day be a different day for the Israelites?

29

MAKE THE DECISION TO
Give Your Hard Season a New Name

And as her soul was departing (for she was dying), she called his name Ben-oni; but his father called him Benjamin.

Genesis 35:18

One of the hardest seasons of my life was when my mom was diagnosed with a brain tumor and given just six months to live. We tried to make the best of things. We still celebrated Mother's Day, an anniversary, and a few birthdays, all while knowing they were our last celebrations with Mom. Which made them all the more bittersweet. We had dance parties in her hospice room, we laughed, we cried, we watched movies together, and we tried to live while she was dying. We were so grateful for the time we had but incredibly sorrowful for the time we felt had been taken from her.

Then, on a Friday morning very early, my mom slipped into eternity. And I truly wondered what it would take for me to be able to say, "It is well with my soul," at the end of my life.

In Genesis 35:18, we're witnesses to the ending of a story. A comparison-filled journey of two sisters, Rachel and Leah, ended in a very sad, sorrowful place: "And as her soul was departing (for she was dying), she called his name Ben-oni; but his father called him Benjamin" (Genesis 35:18).

Rachel's life ends while giving birth to a son. And with her last words, she gave her son the name *Ben-oni*, which means "son of my sorrow." Things were not well with her soul. And her name choice reveals the depth of hurt and pain within her.

But her husband, Jacob (whose own name eventually became Israel), decided to give their son a new name: Benjamin. It meant "son of my right hand, a place of high favor." His son would not live his life with a name representing sorrow.

For sure, this season with my mom was filled with grief. Every day for six months I said goodbye to her a little more. But at the end of her life, I wrestled with the wellness of my soul.

But even in that unwell place of my soul, I knew it was time for me to give this season a new name. Otherwise, things would never shift inside me.

God clearly revealed to me that what I was calling a season of pain, He had given to me as a season of privilege.

It was a privilege to walk day by day with my mom as she crossed into eternity. And now, as I look back and rename that situation, it was a gift, yes, but still wrapped in sorrow.

I don't know why God allows things to happen the way they do. I'm sure Jacob struggled with this, too—wondering as his beloved wife slipped into eternity and he held that baby boy.

At some point, we'll all find ourselves wading through grief. But I know there's a God who gives us a love that redefines our sorrowful seasons.

His Son Jesus is the best example of how God can take pain and rename it something powerful. Like the meaning of Benjamin's new name, Jesus, after a sorrowful season, now sits at the right hand of His Father (Ephesians 1:20–23).

> ## HIS SORROW WAS A SACRIFICE ON THE CROSS, WHICH CHANGED EVERYTHING FOR US.

And because of Jesus, we can walk through hard places and still say, "It is well with my soul." It doesn't mean we'll do it perfectly, smoothly, or even with a smile on our faces. But it means we trust God so much and can make a decision to believe He can rename even the hardest of situations and turn them into something of eternal value.

TAKE THIS DEVOTION DEEPER

Using the space below, think about something in your life that needs to be given a new name by God. Write out a prayer and ask God to reveal something you may not be seeing about that situation.

30

Remember and Retell Others about God's Faithfulness

They remembered that God was their rock, the Most High God their redeemer.

Psalm 78:35

With all our phones, apps, and reminder notifications, it would seem that we really shouldn't forget things. Unfortunately, we still do.

Forgetting isn't a new struggle. Humans are forgetful. And undoubtedly, it'll always be an obstacle for us to overcome.

Psalm 78 was most likely written by Asaph, a servant to King David. Two themes emerge from this text that are very applicable to our generation today: keep telling God's story, and keep remembering God's story.

As a parent, I have a responsibility to teach and remind my children about truth. I can't just tell them once and expect them to remember.

Romans 10:17 tells us that faith comes from hearing.

But the type of hearing referenced here isn't an "I heard you" reaction. It's a place where hearing the faith experiences of others creates a stirring of our own faith. Revelation 12:11 says that our words and testimonies will help others overcome the spiritual battle we all find ourselves in. So, this can't be a one-and-done conversation; it's something that needs to happen again and again in all generations. A huge benefit of retelling is for future generations to believe, but retelling is also for our benefit as well.

Psalm 78:12–72 reminds us to keep looking back on the struggles and victories of those who have gone before us.

Asaph specifically references experiences—from Moses to the Israelites wandering through the wilderness to David—for others to look back on and remember what they went through.

One of the best decisions we can remember to make from this passage is found in Psalm 78:35: "They remembered that God was their rock, the Most High God their redeemer."

They remembered, and so must we. However, if we forget, we can take solace that God knows us and never forgets us (John 10:14). He is always our rock but especially during times of wilderness like the Israelites found themselves in (Deuteronomy 32:4).

AS MANY TIMES AS WE FORGET HIS PRESENCE, HIS PROMISES, HIS TRUTH, AND HIS FAITHFULNESS, HE IS ALWAYS THERE AS OUR REDEEMER (PSALM 19:14).

There are times when my remembering and retelling is a very personal and private process. But, the more I study and then tell what God is teaching me through His Word, the more I personally remember, and almost always, the more others benefit and remember as well.

God's story is a continual process of private remembrance and a consistent public conversation. May we make the decision to always remember and retell.

TAKE THIS DEVOTION DEEPER

If you were standing on a stage right now, speaking to a stadium full of people, what is the one thing you would tell them about how you've experienced God's faithfulness?

Pray and ask God to give you the opportunity today to share that one experience with just one other person.

31

MAKE THE DECISION TO
Draw Near to God

Draw near to God, and He will draw near to you.

James 4:8 HCSB

I t's 3:38 a.m. I stare at the clock, and something inside me whispers, *You should get up.* I toss, turn, and wrestle with my sleep-deprived thoughts for a few minutes before I finally climb out of bed.

I turn on the coffee pot and sit down in the white chair. Opening my journal, these words pour out of my parched soul: "God, I miss You."

Life has been moving at warp speed lately. Work has been busy for both my husband and me, our lives are full, and someone always needs something.

Truth is, I would pay a lot of money for twenty-eight hours in a day.

But mostly, in this stretched season of life, I'm experiencing how "it" happens . . . how people move far from God.

It's not always intentional:

Someone in our family is sick, so church is missed.

Work has to start earlier the next morning, leaving no time for quiet prayer.

Bodies need exercise, so reading the Bible gets pushed aside.

Meals must be prepared, so worship becomes secondary.

Reports and projects have to be finished. . . .

You get the idea. The list goes on and on of what can keep us from the closeness of God.

I understand these struggles all too well. And I'm finding there is a great danger in these stretched times of life.

> **WE CAN MISS BEING WITH GOD, BUT WE ALSO CAN MISS THE MOVEMENT GOD IS DOING IN OUR LIVES. MISSING GOD (EITHER WAY) IS TRAGIC AND THREATENING TO OUR SOULS, WHICH LONG TO THRIVE WITH GOD.**

Recognizing how much I've missed God, I'm taking some time to reflect on this struggle and make the decision to draw closer to Him. I'm burdened but also hopeful in the words He is breathing during these soul-stretching moments.

Maybe you too feel that tug in your heart, pulling you back to Him. I share these three things we can do to move toward the decision to draw closer to the heart of God.

1. Find our God-space

Even if it means it's 3:38 a.m. When life feels busy, stretched, and chaotic, I can stay open to the Spirit's prompting on my heart to create God-space.

Obviously, 3:38 a.m. won't always work for me, so I do need to be intentional about scheduling time with God. Finding the moments of time when we can fully be with Him is important. "Draw near to God, and He will draw near to you" (James 4:8 HCSB).

2. Experience the awe of God

The colors of the sky on the drive into the office . . . experience them. The sun warming our skin on a chilly day . . . experience it. Giggles from children, the way someone we love smiles, the praise of God's people . . . experience them all.

May these moments remind us what it's like to be fully alive and connected to Someone much bigger than ourselves. "Let all the earth fear the LORD; let all the inhabitants of the world stand in awe of him!" (Psalm 33:8).

3. Have ears that listen {always}

The prompting in your heart to slow down, to breathe in the moment . . . listen to it. A nudge on your soul to say no when you really want to say yes . . . listen to it (or vice versa).

May we not want to just dream about the promises God has for our life, but want to live them by listening to His voice, always. "And after the fire came a gentle whisper" (1 Kings 19:12 NIV).

There is always an opportunity in the midst of our busy lives to be aware of God. As we find Him, experience Him, and listen for Him, our intentional steps will always lead us closer to His presence.

TAKE THIS DEVOTION DEEPER

Which of these three things challenges you the most today?

Pray this with me:

> *Lord, please help me to be intentional with my steps toward You. I can't always control the things around me, but I know with Your guidance I can still draw close to You when life feels so stretched. Amen.*

32

MAKE THE DECISION TO
Trust the Slow Work of God

The LORD is good to those who wait for him, to the soul who seeks him.

Lamentations 3:25

Just outside my office door hangs a sign that says, *Above all, trust in the slow work of God.* I look at it each day as a reminder to believe God is working even when I don't see progress.

Sometimes it feels like God is moving so fast I can barely keep up. And other times it feels so slow it makes me wonder if it's just too loud in heaven. Can He hear me? Does He care? When is the answer, relief, or sign of hope coming?

The slowness of God isn't something we tend to embrace. But perhaps it's where the greatest change, breakthrough, or miracle will come from.

> **THE SLOW WORK OF GOD IS NOT NECESSARILY A PLACE OF REST, BUT IT IS A PLACE OF RESTORATION.**

Almost ten years ago my husband and I purchased a foreclosed farm. It was a disaster and needed a lot of restoration. It's been a slow process. Sometimes you can't really see the progress because it's hidden from eyesight.

Like the time we had to spend almost our entire savings to make the toilets flush again. When people would stop by and ask for an update on what we'd done recently, I'd sarcastically say, "Come here, let me show you how the toilet flushes!"

But other times it's been so dramatically fast, like when we knocked down a wall in the kitchen, people stopping by would notice it right away.

Our process with God can be so similar. But the slowness is where we tend to wrestle the most.

Slow work doesn't mean you don't sleep your way there. You don't sit your way there. You work. Hard and often slow. Focused and with a plan. It's painful and expensive. But it's doable when you just take it slow and steady.

So much of the book of Lamentations is filled with sorrow and sadness. But then there are verses like 3:25 that shine a glimmer of light into these dark places in Scripture.

Theologian Philip Ryken said this about this specific verse: "There are times when the only thing a sufferer can do is wait for God. But waiting is good because God is worth waiting for."[1]

I love that so much. I need to be reminded of this each day. So, yes, may we make the decision to trust the slow work of our God.

TAKE THIS DEVOTION DEEPER

Write out James 5:7–8:

Make a list of the areas you have seen God work quickly:

Now make a list of the areas you have seen God work slowly:

33

MAKE THE DECISION TO
Make a Sound That Matters

So that with one mind and one voice you may glorify the God and Father of our Lord Jesus Christ.

Romans 15:6 NIV

One of my first jobs was at a little nursing home where I helped take care of patients in the Alzheimer's unit. While caring for people battling such a difficult disease created many challenges, there was also a lot of laughter.

Mostly because of a sweet, tiny lady named Bunny. Bunny slid her walker through the hallways, singing all kinds of songs. Some of the other caregivers told me Bunny was one of the original munchkins from *The Wizard of Oz*. I believed it, too, as she was something incredible!

As Bunny would party through the hallways, the other patients echoed her melody, and amusing sounds filled the air. As I'd pass Bunny on my rounds, I'd look at her and say, "Sing it, girl!" And then, she'd take it up a notch and we'd laugh until our sides ached.

Bunny's sounds made everyone's experience at the nursing home much brighter.

Here's the thing: while it's true not everyone can sing, we all have some type of voice flowing from our lives.

But is it a harmonious sound, or is it just noise? Because there is a difference.

One definition for noise is "any sound that is undesired and interferes with one's hearing of something."[1] When we go back further, we learn the word *noise* originated from the Latin word *nausea* meaning "seasickness."

Using those definitions, noise is annoying and no one wants to hear it. It's often hard to think over the noise. Ever hear a momma say to a room full of kids banging on toys, "Quit making all that noise!"? It's distracting at best, and downright painful at worst.

Bunny's singing wasn't perfect, and sometimes it got really loud, but it always accomplished the same thing: joy.

It was a sound that needed to be heard.

I like Romans 15:6 (NIV) because it paints a clear picture of what it means to represent the sound of God: "So that with one mind and one voice you may glorify the God and Father of our Lord Jesus Christ."

> **THE SOUND OF GOD IS ONE OF PEACE, JOY, GENTLENESS, AND HARMONY.**
> **IT'S ALSO A SOUND THAT UNIFIES US RATHER THAN DIVIDES US.**

I think noise would be everything opposite: hate, conflict, and rudeness.

So, here's the question I'm asking myself each day about what's flowing from me: *Is this a sound I'm making today, or is it just noise?*

It's a good question to help us make the wise decision to make a sound that matters. You have a powerful sound ready to flow through you. So go . . . make that sound loud and clear.

TAKE THIS DEVOTION DEEPER

Read 1 Corinthians 13:1.

What does it mean to you personally to make a sound that reflects God?

34

Always Be Ready to
Share the Gospel

How beautiful on the mountains are the feet of the messenger who brings good news, the good news of peace and salvation, the news that the God of Israel reigns!

Isaiah 52:7 NLT

I stood in a field with two Kenyan pastors, resting after we'd traveled long distances.

For five days we'd gone from hut to hut sharing the life-changing truth of Jesus. We prayed and listened to others, and I cried tears of disbelief over the devastating poverty.

In our short time together, these pastors taught me new definitions of boldness, courage, and passion for others to know the Lord. They would often walk thirty miles just to have the opportunity to share about Jesus with one family. Sometimes I barely even want to say hello to my thirty-feet-away neighbor who desperately needs God.

Yes, these men were living examples of Isaiah 52:7 (NLT): "How beautiful on the mountains are the feet of the messenger who brings good news, the good news of peace and salvation, the news that the God of Israel reigns!"

Biblical commentaries tell us the messenger in this passage was bringing good news to the Jews who had been enslaved for a long time. The messenger could be seen as he ran on the distant hills toward the people who'd been in captivity. He came with a message of great hope and joy to tell them they were free! Free from bondage, free from despair.

There is another message that was brought to all people, including you, me, my friends in Africa, and the whole world: the good news of the coming Messiah, Jesus.

THAT GOOD NEWS IS ABOUT HIS BIRTH AND HIS DEATH AND RESURRECTION. IT GIVES US THE HOPE THAT CAME TO EARTH AS A BABY, DIED AS A MAN, AND ROSE AS OUR SAVIOR TO OFFER US ETERNAL LIFE.

It's the same news the two men trekked all around the dusty Kenyan land to share. For days after I returned home, the passion of these pastors consumed my thoughts. And brought to life the call I have to share the Word of God—not just with people in other countries, but with those around me.

I learned so much from my Kenyan friends. I may not walk hundreds of miles to take the good news to others, but I can drive across town to minister joy to the homeless. I can cross the street to speak with my neighbor about how Jesus can set us free from the captivity of anxiety. And I can share the peace people are looking for.

But it is a decision to do so. And the wisest-in-the-Lord people I have met are some of the boldest spreaders of the gospel. They feel no fear or shame in sharing the hope they have found in Jesus.

I have found the days I tell God, *I'm available, use me,* are the days He seems to open up doors of opportunity to share the gospel. Tell God right now that you're making this decision to be ready to share, and ask Him to use you today.

TAKE THIS DEVOTION DEEPER

What does it look like for you today to share the gospel with someone?

Sometimes it helps us be prepared to share the gospel with someone by writing out our story of how we encountered God. I encourage you to do that, but I also encourage you to be ready to share God's faithfulness in your story today. We should have a testimony each day of what God is doing in and through us.

Use the space below to write out some of the current ways God has met you:

35

MAKE THE DECISION TO

Be the Peacemaker

Blessed are the peacemakers, for they will be called children of God.

Matthew 5:9 NIV

There's a story of an eight-year-old boy who once wrote his pastor a letter. "Dear Pastor, I know God wants us to live in peace with everybody, but He never met my sister. Sincerely, William."

I bet you and I could write similar letters. There's always someone who seems to get under our skin, isn't there? In a world filled with irritating people and problem makers, being able to bring peace in the midst of it all can feel impossible.

Because we are born into a world of sin, we don't always have automatic peacemaking reactions. One of our responses may be to engage our defense mechanisms and retaliate when provoked. Or we may turn inward and shut down, not seeking to work things out. This is why parents and schoolteachers struggle to train children to resolve their issues with each other peaceably.

God modeled the right way to seek peace. When we offended God with our disobedience, He took the initiative to reconcile our relationship through His Son's death on the cross. Through Jesus's sacrifice and salvation, I'm no longer subject to my defensive reactions or to shutting down. Instead, I have access to His peace, which makes being a peacemaker possible.

Recently, while going through some conflicts with people, I read Matthew 5:9: "Blessed are the peacemakers . . ."

When I first read this, I thought, *If I will just memorize this verse, boom . . . I will be a peacemaker*. So I did. Big surprise . . . I wasn't a peacemaker the next time conflict arose.

I recognized that I needed to have a deeper understanding of what it means to be a peacemaker, so I dug into Scripture.

To some, *peace* can be defined as harmony, security, and rest. These words remind me of the things Jesus brings into our lives. Because we follow Him, He gives us the ability to make peace. When we do, He promises we "will be called children of God" (Matthew 5:9 NIV). We can be a representation of the peace He gives.

> **WHEN JESUS SAID WE ARE BLESSED WHEN WE BRING PEACE, IT IS BECAUSE BEING A PEACEMAKER ALLOWS US AS HIS CHILDREN TO REPRESENT THE DEPTH OF WHO HE IS.**

Some people will go to great lengths to prove themselves right. Pride and arrogance convince them that laying aside differences is a sign of weakness. But if we can catch God's vision of what it looks like to be a peacemaker—to bring harmony, security, and rest to a difficult situation—it will allow us to feel secure and at rest in the midst of conflict. We can stand confident as children of God.

As we let go of petty stuff, we are peacemakers. When we are the first to say, "I'm sorry," we give peace. When we talk calmly rather than yell, we bring peace to the situation. By learning to give peace the way we receive peace from Jesus, His peace flows through our lives.

Making the decision to be a peacemaker is challenging and may not come naturally. But may we be reminded today that in every conflict we can bring peaceful resolutions. We can make the decision to bring harmony, security, and rest because Jesus's death and resurrection gave that power to us.

TAKE THIS DEVOTION DEEPER

Read Philippians 4:7. What is a situation in your life you need God's peace over? Pray this verse and ask the Holy Spirit to help you guard your heart and mind in that situation. Look for ways you can be a peacemaker.

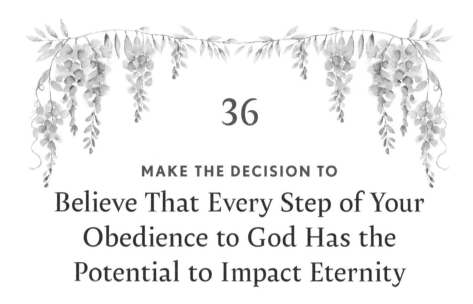

36

Believe That Every Step of Your Obedience to God Has the Potential to Impact Eternity

And let us not grow weary of doing good, for in due season we will reap, if we do not give up.

Galatians 6:9

I confess, as a lover of telling and writing stories, I often find myself drafting the ending to certain circumstances in my life. Sometimes the ending I write in my head is beautiful, and sometimes it isn't.

But a lot of times my endings are wrong. Especially when it comes to situations I'm trusting God with.

I tend to think how I see a situation must be how it is. But often flying in a plane gives me the opportunity to look out the window and try to grasp God's perspective over the earth. It is way beyond what we can see from down below.

Our physical sight has limitations. We can only see so far and so wide. And often our physical sight transfers to our spiritual sight.

But God is full of mystery, with a perspective beyond anything we can comprehend. So when we allow Him to write the endings to our stories, they often end up being something more than we could ever ask or imagine (Ephesians 3:20).

In the book of Ruth, we can see a beautiful ending begin to unfold from what began as a tragic story. Boaz takes Ruth as his wife. Ruth and Naomi move into a new season of restoration. And this would have been a great place for this story to end!

But the last verse of Ruth 4 tells us the most amazing part of this story: "Obed the father of Jesse, and Jesse the father of David" (Ruth 4:22 NIV).

In Ruth, we read that the elders of Bethlehem offered a blessing over Boaz and Ruth. It was a blessing that their offspring would leave a legacy pointing to the building of the kingdom of God.

Ruth 4:13 is the actual fulfillment of this blessing. Scripture says Ruth and Boaz had a baby boy named Obed. And Obed grew up and became the father of a boy named Jesse. Jesse grew up and became the father of a man named David. And David is incredibly important because Jesus is described as being the son of David, meaning He descended from David's generational line (Matthew 1:1–16).

Obed is this generational link between Perez and David mentioned in Ruth 4:18–22. His genealogical line points backward to God's faithfulness through Perez and forward to God's fulfillment through David.

But here's something to think about . . .

While living on this earth, Ruth never knew that Jesus Christ would come through her generational line. The fulfillment of Jesus's coming to earth would be many, many, many years later.

God's providential plan for Ruth is a beautiful likeness of what God is doing through you and me.

> ## THERE IS A GENERATIONAL LINE FLOWING THROUGH YOU AND ME THAT GOD WANTS TO IMPACT IN THE NAME OF JESUS CHRIST.

Like Obed, our lives also point to two things: Jesus came, and Jesus will return. We are links in this generational process.

Galatians 6:9 offers us a promise of what can happen if we make the decision to believe every step of our obedience to God can become a harvest. A harvest like Ruth's. We may not ever comprehend fully until we arrive in heaven, because God's perspective is beyond what we can see here and now.

But it's going to be worth it. May we make this decision today and every day. Because wisdom truly is understanding that our lives reach beyond today.

TAKE THIS DEVOTION DEEPER

Read all of Ruth 4.

What is something you see in your life today that has the potential to impact future generations and direct them toward Jesus?

How do you need to steward that situation well?

37

MAKE THE DECISION TO

Seek Out Common Sense and Discernment from the Lord

> My child, don't lose sight of common sense and discernment.
> Hang on to them, for they will refresh your soul.
>
> Proverbs 3:21–22 NLT

Women are ridiculous," I said to my husband as I crawled into bed, tears dripping. He gave me an agreeable stare since he had no words to console my aching heart.

I'd just learned a friend had lied to me. It was about something senseless, which just made it worse. As the hours ticked by, I wrestled through troubling thoughts.

Why would she lie about THAT?

Were we ever really friends?

The combination of hurt and middle-of-the-night thinking was toxic, forming a very self-centered attitude in me. I decided I no longer had room in my life to deal with someone who had lied to me. So in my heart, I just unfriended this friend.

I have other people I can be friends with, I thought as I drifted off to sleep.

The next morning I realized how my emotions had distorted my perceptions. It concerned me how quickly I was willing to write off this friend, since we had been through a lot together. And I really did value our relationship.

So I considered the emotions swirling in my heart.

In our culture today, it's easy to sit behind screens while we reject the reality of many things, including friendships.

A profile on Facebook could say someone has nine hundred "friends." Social media can convince us we have hundreds of people in our corner. But in reality, we don't have nine hundred friends we could call in the midst of a crisis or even go meet for a cup of coffee.

And that *unfriend* or *unfollow* button is mighty tempting when someone hurts us. But the truth is, ending a relationship is much more complex than the way social media convinces me it can happen—as easily as clicking an icon.

Social media is a relational tool, but it's not a relational reality.

More than ever, we need to see our relationships through the lens of reality, and this verse helps me do this: "My child, don't lose sight of common sense and discernment. Hang on to them, for they will refresh your soul" (Proverbs 3:21–22 NLT).

> GOD HAS GIVEN US TWO TRUSTWORTHY FILTERS
> TO HELP US SEE THINGS AS THEY REALLY ARE:
> COMMON SENSE AND DISCERNMENT.

But it will be our decision, in the heat of emotional moments, to use them both.

In this situation with my friend, common sense reminded me: *You don't have nine hundred friends, but you do have a handful of people you can really count on. And you need to cultivate those relationships through good times and bad.*

Discernment said: *Your friend is human. At the core of her heart, she cares about you and didn't mean to hurt you.*

We will always be susceptible to flawed perceptions in our relationships. But when we hang on to the realities God offers us through seeking common sense and discernment, I believe we will be much wiser with our perceptions.

When deciding to use God's Word rather than our emotions as our filter, it allows us to work through hurtful issues with people without completely writing them off.

TAKE THIS DEVOTION DEEPER

Look up these two verses. What wisdom do they offer you about seeking out common sense and discernment with God?

1 Corinthians 13:12

1 John 3:2

38

MAKE THE DECISION TO

See Things for What
They Really Are

> We do not dare to classify or compare ourselves with some who commend themselves. When they measure themselves by themselves and compare themselves with themselves, they are not wise.
>
> 2 Corinthians 10:12 NIV

Have you ever had a situation that ended up not being anything like it appeared to be?

I was off on an adventure with my friend Amy. A junking adventure. You know, sorting through what some consider trash and turning it into home decor treasure.

But our adventure on an old farm led me in a completely different decorating direction. Because somehow, a sweet baby donkey ended up coming home with me.

Only problem was, I discovered donkeys can't live alone. So I did some negotiating and ended up with not one but *two* donkeys. And according to the man selling me these donkeys, the girl was pregnant.

Basically, it was a BOGO (buy one get one) deal, and I was thrilled.

Since my husband and I are first-generation farmers (read: we have no idea what we're doing), surprisingly we found out donkeys are pregnant for eleven to fourteen months!

And so began Baby Donkey Watch.

For months, I went outside each day to love on Helen and her ever-growing belly. I posted pictures on social media, and everyone became excited about this coming baby donkey.

But eleven months went by, then twelve, thirteen, fourteen months . . . and still no baby donkey. Yet Helen kept getting bigger and bigger and bigger.

Puzzled, I called a donkey expert to come figure out this situation. I explained things, and he gave Helen a quick once-over. Then he said to me (in his deep southern accent), "Ma'am, I'm sorry to tell you this, but that donkey isn't pregnant."

WHAT?

Oh. My. Word.

I could not believe it. I mean, I had felt Helen's stomach move! And why was she getting wider and wider?

Things are not always as they seem.

Honestly, when I think about one of the greatest struggles of my life—comparison—this is a truth I've had to pour into my heart over and over.

Comparison tricks me into looking at what others have and who they are, and I wonder if somehow they measure higher in God's eyes than I do. When I look at others' success, it's easy to fall into a destructive mindset. And as Paul wrote in 2 Corinthians 10:12, comparison makes us unwise.

"We do not dare to classify or compare ourselves with some who commend themselves. When they measure themselves by themselves and compare themselves with themselves, *they are not wise*" (2 Corinthians 10:12, emphasis mine).

Wisdom helps us see beyond every seemingly perfect situation and know there's usually another story being written. That story is rarely told.

> **THE WORLD LOVES TO SHOUT**
> **ABOUT SUCCESS,**
> **BUT WE SELDOM SPEAK**
> **OF OUR SECRET SORROWS.**
> **AND COMPARISON IS OFTEN**
> **A QUIET, SORROWFUL PLACE**
> **WE DON'T INVITE OTHERS INTO.**

Helen's stomach grew and grew because she was just . . . well, eating a lot. Her new home is a pasture with maybe too much grass to feed on. So, dreadfully, I had to pop open my phone and craft a social media post to fill in the entire Baby Donkey Watch fan base of this outcome.

People were disappointed, but mostly just laughing with us, not at us.

And I know it's a super trivial example, but each time I look at Helen, I remember things aren't always as they seem. And I want to be wise when I look at the world around me so that comparison doesn't compromise the unique story God is writing through my life.

It's a wise decision to make and keep making.

TAKE THIS DEVOTION DEEPER

List a few areas comparison has tried to write another story in your life:

Why do you think Paul warned us about this struggle? What could have been some of the comparison struggles during biblical times?

39

MAKE THE DECISION TO

Ask for Help
When You Need It

When Moses' hands grew heavy, they took a stone and put it under him, and he sat down on it. Then Aaron and Hur supported his hands, one on one side and one on the other so that his hands remained steady until the sun went down.

Exodus 17:12 HCSB

We were sitting in gray chairs next to white walls, listening to the hum of the air-conditioning unit. My legs crossed. His arms folded.

The memories of twelve years of arguments flashed before my eyes. The pride, the anger, the selfishness, the cold silence.

How does happily-ever-after end up like this? And when did we decide we couldn't ask for help?

I know how and when. It happened when we decided to stuff our feelings and put Band-Aids over deep wounds because it seemed more visually appealing than an exposed injury.

Years had passed, and we kept going until neither of us could take it any longer.

And now we sat in these gray chairs next to these white walls. Our last effort. The words I couldn't say all those years before spilled from my lips ... "We just need help."

Help was offered, and I could finally breathe again. It was almost too late ...

A few days later, I got one of those early morning phone calls. The kind of early morning call you know once you answer, your life will never be the same. An attempted suicide from someone close.

A soul who also wasn't able to say, "I need help." And I'm troubled by another almost-too-late cry for help I had no idea was being stifled.

Each day we pass by people who, like Moses, are becoming incredibly weary.

Moses was in the midst of a battle for the Lord. With the staff of God in his hand, he noticed that each time he let his arms down, the enemy advanced. But each time he held his arms up, the Israelite army advanced.

Moses had to keep his arms up for the victory, but he eventually grew weary and couldn't do it on his own. Two people came alongside Moses to hold up his arms for just a little longer, and the Israelites defeated the Amalekites.

Two things challenge me from this story:

First, the ability to say, "I just need help."

The Bible doesn't say Moses asked for help, but I imagine he did—either verbally or with a "Come here, come quick!" look or motion with his head. Contrary to what my soul screams, these are not words of weakness, but rather strength. They mean I'm not ready to give up: I want to keep going. I just need a little help. Vulnerability is one of the first things we look for in other people but the last thing we are willing to show ourselves.

Second, the ability to see those around me who need me to help hold up their arms.

> **MAYBE ONE OF THE GREATEST PRAYERS WE CAN PRAY IS TO ASK GOD TO SHOW US WHO IT IS THAT NEEDS HELP ... OUR HELP.**

Sure, it's risky to stand beside people who are ready to give up, but I believe this is one of the greatest opportunities for our own personal growth. Compassion is a powerful form of strength.

I want to be a woman who lives to see victory in others and myself. When my arms feel heavy, I want to make a decision to ask for help. And when I see others' arms falling, I want to quickly look for stones I can place under them.

TAKE THIS DEVOTION DEEPER

If it's hard for you to ask for help, why?

What is something you need help with today? Who can you reach out to?

Who is someone who might need your help?

40

Keep Finding Ways to Make Wise Decisions

How much better to get wisdom than gold, to get insight rather than silver!

Proverbs 16:16 NIV

I t wasn't the best introduction to mentoring. Our church was doing a mentorship program, and as a young wife and mom, I knew I needed someone to speak into my life. So I signed up. Our first meeting as mentor/mentee went great, or so I thought.

But for a variety of reasons, my mentor stood me up twice, and I became incredibly discouraged with the thought of pursuing another mentor.

But a few months later I would meet a woman who would step into my story and become part of the process that God was leading me through to learn what it means to pursue godly wisdom.

Over the years there have been times when I didn't need a friend to tell me she thought I was amazing. I needed someone to push me toward being a better wife and mom. I needed someone who would help me understand how to honor my mom as she died. I needed someone to read something I had written and say things like, "You may need to look at this Scripture again and make sure you are using it correctly."

And God sent several mentors in my life to help me. He will do the same for you. But the process of seeking and finding wisdom isn't one that just happens. This last decision is one that will continue on and on if we surround ourselves with Truth and wise people.

Here are four ways to make wise decisions, with verses, to help you keep living out this process with God:

1. Ask God to begin to give you the spirit of discernment. Discernment is a gift God gives us and one we should ask for help in developing each day.

   "Who is wise? Let them realize these things. Who is discerning? Let them understand. The ways of the LORD are right; the righteous walk in them, but the rebellious stumble in them" (Hosea 14:9 NIV).

2. Ask someone you think is wise to mentor you. There's something intimidating about calling someone up and asking them to be our mentor, and mentoring takes commitment. There doesn't have to be an official title. Just find someone wiser than you and ask questions.

   "Wisdom is with the aged, and understanding in length of days" (Job 12:12).

3. Never take someone's word for it when it comes to understanding biblical wisdom. Also, do not trust every article or website you come across online.

   "Dear friends, do not believe every spirit, but test the spirits to see whether they are from God, because many false prophets have gone out into the world" (1 John 4:1 NIV).

4. Give your wisdom freely to others. If I've come to understand anything in the last few years of my life, it's that people are more

interested in my process than they are in my outcome. The more of God's wisdom you take in, the more you must be willing to give it away to others.

> "Remember this: Whoever sows sparingly will also reap sparingly, and whoever sows generously will also reap generously" (2 Corinthians 9:6 NIV).

Our journey through these forty decisions has come to an end here in this devotional book. But this is just the foundational building block for wisdom in your life. And if you get to the point in the next few weeks, months, or even years where you feel like you need to spend some time rebuilding wisdom, I'll still be right here on these pages with you.

> ## KEEP MAKING DECISIONS EACH DAY THAT HELP YOU BECOME A LITTLE ... WISER.

TAKE THIS DEVOTION DEEPER

Who is someone in your life who gives you godly wisdom?

Over the last forty decisions you've made, which one do you feel has impacted you the most?

How will you keep finding wisdom to help you become wiser?

NOTES

Chapter 9: Make the Decision to Remember Who Your Battle Is Against

1, Billy Graham, "Hopeless, Yet There Is Hope," 1975, Albuquerque, New Mexico, Billy Graham Evangelistic Association, August 3, 2020, https://billygraham.org/video/hopeless-yet-there-is-hope/.

Chapter 10: Make the Decision to Look for the Goodness of God

1. *Oxford English Dictionary*, s.v. "confirmation bias," https://www.oed.com/search/dictionary/?scope=Entries&q=confirmation+bias.

Chapter 32: Make the Decision to Trust the Slow Work of God

1. Philip Graham Ryken, *Jeremiah and Lamentations: From Sorrow to Hope* (Wheaton: Crossway, 2001), 761.

Chapter 33: Make the Decision to Make a Sound That Matters

1. *Merriam-Webster*, s.v. "noise," https://www.merriam-webster.com/dictionary/noise.

NICKI KOZIARZ is a bestselling author and speaker. She speaks nationally at conferences, retreats, and meetings, and hosts her own podcast, *Lessons from the Farm*. A Bible teacher at heart, Nicki inspires others to become the best version of who God created them to be through the Scriptures. Nicki, her husband, and their family run a small farm just outside of Charlotte, North Carolina, they affectionately call The Fixer Upper Farm. Learn more at NickiKoziarz.com.